THE LIFE LEADERSHIP TEXTBOOK

BUILDING COMPENSATED COMMUNITIES

New York Times Bestselling Authors
CHRIS BRADY AND ORRIN WOODWARD

Obstaclés Press and the Obstaclés logo are trademarks of LIFE
Leadership.

Eighth Edition, June 2014 (formerly published as: *The LIFE
Team Builder's Textbook* and *The Team Builder's Textbook*)

Published by:

Obstaclés Press
4072 Market Place Dr.
Flint, MI 48507

Scripture quotations marked "KJV" are taken from the Holy Bible,
King James Version, Cambridge, 1769.

lifeleadership.com

ISBN 978-0-9904243-2-1

Cover design and layout by Norm Williams, nwa-inc.com
Comic illustrations by Sean Catron

Printed in the United States of America

Our greatest fear should not be of failure, but of succeeding at something that doesn't really matter.
—D. L. Moody

IN MEMORY OF JACKIE LEWIS

ACKNOWLEDGMENTS

We would like to say thank you to our wives, Terri Brady and Laurie Woodward, for unyielding love, support, understanding, and flexibility.

Thanks are also due to Rob Hallstrand and the entire staff at Obstaclés Press. We want to thank Norm Williams for artwork, Bill Rousseau for project management, and Deborah Brady and Michelle Turner for editing and book production oversight. Thank you also to Ryan Renz and his staff of professional media specialists for excellent work day in and day out. In addition, we wish to express our heartfelt gratitude for the contributions of each of the LIFE Leadership founders, Tim and Amy Marks, George and Jill Guzzardo, Bill (and Jackie) Lewis, Claude and Lana Hamilton, Dan and Lisa Hawkins, and Rob Hallstrand, as well as Holger and Lindsey Spiewak, Curtis and Debbie Spolar, Felmar and Sandra Montenegro, Wayne and Raylene MacNamara, and Chris and Danaé Mattis. You are incredible leaders, and it's a pleasure to be in business with you.

And as always and in everything, we give all the honor and glory to our Lord and Savior Jesus Christ. Everything we have and will ever accomplish is by His grace.

CONTENTS

Contents

Contents

INTRODUCTION

The Internet Age is upon us; there is no arguing it. The Industrial Age is over, and the Information Age is here. The old world and the old ways are gone. The diagram below gives a brief overview of how new ages displace old ones and how this process is happening faster than it ever has before.

AGRARIAN AGE   INDUSTRIAL AGE   INFORMATION AGE

World-renowned economist Paul Zane Pilzer said in *The Next Millionaires*, "The Internet represents one of the greatest economic revolutions in history—and it's just getting started. The impact of the Internet, which is even now only in its infancy, can only be compared to the invention of writing, which created the birth of civilization, and the printing press, which created industrialization." Statistics are certainly readily available to support Pilzer's claims. There are more people online than ever before. There are more people *shopping* online than ever before. And the amount the average electronic commerce shopper is spending continually goes up.

Pilzer goes on to say, "*The Next Millionaires* explains how you can become one of them—especially if you are in direct selling, technology, home-based business, product distribution, or an emerging trillion-dollar industry like wellness."

Michael Dell, billionaire founder of Dell Computers, gave a speech to the Detroit Economic Club in November of 1999. In that talk, he outlined the importance of being in business and capitalizing on the enormous trends of the Internet. Dell stipulated that to be in business and not be involved in the explosiveness of the Information Age would be to miss the greatest business opportunity of our lifetime. Further, Dell explained the concept of developing "communities" of loyal, enthusiastic customers *online*. Anybody can build a website, and nearly everyone has. Anybody can invest some money and fill a warehouse with products to sell through that website, and many companies have. But it takes something more to develop a base of customers, or in Dell's words, a "community" of shoppers that will return to the website again and again. Conventional advertising techniques have proven largely ineffective. More contemporary approaches such as banner ads and referral kickbacks have also performed poorly. For these reasons, despite an exploding customer base, most companies have actually *failed* at developing significant web traffic for their products!

Something more is needed, something that will build and sustain enthusiasm and loyalty on the part of the customer, something that will bring them back repeatedly and cause them to bring their friends. That "something" is called *business ownership*, or a "piece of the action." With the enormous cost reductions possible through the Internet, such as elimination of the retail store, advertising, and several distribution steps, there is ample revenue that can be shared among a body of owners to reward them for developing a customer base. Some have taken to calling this the Consumer Rebellion. Such a plan brings the idea of Internet business down to the level of the individual. In a nutshell, that is the *opportunity* side of the business: a chance to build communities of people who share a financial interest in developing electronic commerce. That opportunity has proven to work well. It requires very little money to initiate, operate, or expand. It involves no complicated licensing or qualification procedures. Quitting one's current means of employment is unnecessary, and bank loans or building mortgages are not required. The upside is unlimited, while the entrance requirements are extremely low. And it is an opportunity available to anyone with basic ambition and an eagerness to learn.

Having a great *opportunity* is the **first component** of wealth. One simply cannot create wealth where no opportunity exists. Why is it that the most inventions and patents, research papers, and technological advancements come out of free countries? Why is there almost a ratio that shows that the freer the country, the more prolific the opportunities? And why is it that those same countries are the wealthiest? The reason is because opportunity must be available before wealth can be created. Former Ohio Congressman Bob McEwen says, "The greater the freedom, the greater the wealth."

The **second component** of wealth is *proper thinking*. Opportunity is one thing; taking advantage of it is another. It takes knowledge, wisdom, and experience to build and sustain wealth. As an example, consider a lottery. When an individual wins a state-sponsored lottery, generally there is a large sum of money at stake. Without any special abilities, character development, or specialized knowledge and experience, an individual has suddenly received enormous financial means. Certainly, at least for the winning individual, the lottery proves to be a great opportunity. But without the proper thinking, without experience and wisdom, wealth is nearly always fleeting. Many, many lottery winners not only squander their winnings but end up filing for bankruptcy! This means that the new onrush of funds came in and hijacked the old, pre-existing funds! As this demonstrates, opportunity itself, even if enormous, is not able to create wealth; for wealth to be created, experience and knowledge must accompany opportunity.

LIFE Leadership offers the very rare chance to have both opportunity and wealth thinking. This book is about this second component. Regardless of how great LIFE Leadership is, you must know how to utilize, build, and sustain it for the full potential to be realized in *your* life. Building communities of people associated with online commerce of life-changing information is not a common skill. If it were, other providers of personal development and leadership materials would already be doing it successfully. They have certainly tried! But community building is a special expertise, one at which LIFE Leadership has proven especially adept by helping business owners lead their field for years. Tens of thousands of business owners throughout the world plug into the LIFE Training Marketing System on a regular basis to learn the expertise of building communities. Audio recordings, books, pamphlets, videos, downloads, a complete Marketing System, seminars, and national conventions comprise a training strategy with proven, systematic results. It is structured and presented from two very important levels:

1. Principles
2. Specifics (methods or techniques)

To build a community of people through which the sale of life-changing information takes place and to establish a profitable business, *both* principles and specifics must be learned. The old axiom is: "Methods are many; principles are few. Methods always change, but principles never do." The LIFE Training Marketing System comprises both aspects of education by embodying principles that are timeless and methods that are timely.

This book is similarly structured. You will not only uncover the principles required to build and sustain LIFE Leadership profitably, but you will also become familiar with specific techniques that work in the field today. *The LIFE Leadership Textbook* organizes the key concepts and areas of expertise LIFE Leadership has developed and discovered over the years into an easily readable and accessible format. It comprises the overall framework of building a community and makes references to additional training aids that can provide deeper understanding of particular concepts or techniques.

The story is told of a young man who graduated from high school and took a job in a sporting goods store. One day, a wealthy customer entered and purchased a large sum of items with cash. The young man decided to assist the customer as he transported his goods out to the parking lot. Along the way, the curious young man posed the question, "How do I get to be successful like you someday?"

The customer stopped and looked the young man over for a moment, never before having been asked a question that wise. After considering his reply, the customer said, "First, determine what you want in life. Second, find someone who has accomplished it and learn all you can from them. Third, go do what they did." With that, the customer got into his car and drove off. The young man never even got the man's name, but he did get a piece of advice that made him wealthy.

While most of us know what we want in life, it becomes very difficult to find someone who has achieved success and is interested in teaching us how he or she accomplished it. This book takes care of that step. It shows and teaches a clearly marked path to success and significance, one that involves *Having Fun, Making Money, and Making a Difference* in people's lives, all while exploiting the enormous potential of the Internet and the Information Age. All that is left for you to do is apply it.

CHAPTER 1

DREAMS

THE POWER OF *WHY*

Carl Sandburg said, "Nothing happens without first a dream." If we don't know what we're shooting for, we'll probably never hit it. Said another way, if we aim at nothing, we will hit it with amazing accuracy.

The first step in building a strong and profitable business is to understand why you're doing it in the first place. It seems so elementary that many people will say, "I know what I want; teach me how to get it!" or "You teach me how to make the money, and I'll know how to spend it." But success doesn't work that way. Knowing *why* is much more important than knowing *how*.

Don't get us wrong; this book is all about teaching the *how*. But success can never be obtained without a strong enough *why*. The reason for this is that the *why* provides the energy and motivation required to execute the *how*. "Not me," some say, "I'm self-motivated!" Wrong again. Normally the person that makes a statement like that has very little success in life. They haven't needed motivation because they haven't accomplished anything! Rest assured; true success will require a strong *why*.

Dreams

Both of us have a professional background in engineering. Nowhere, ever, were we taught to make use of the word *dream*. There was no Dream 101 course. There was no way to calculate the strength of a dream. There was no need to even know the word in order to build parts for cars. Besides, any engineer worth his salt knows that such talk is hokey. Engineers (and probably those in most professions) don't talk about dreams. Instead, they talk about goals, objectives, strategies, action items, deliverables,

1

standards, and other exciting corporate buzzwords—but never the word *dream*.

We are quite certain most people share a similar opinion about dreams. But this book isn't about *most people*. It's about people who want to excel and succeed; it's about people who want to live incredible lives; it's about people who choose to rise above the lure of mediocrity and strive for excellence. Because of that, it is important to consider not what *most people* do with the concept of dreams but what *extraordinary people* think about dreams.

Author and speaker Norman Vincent Peale said, "To achieve anything significant, everyone needs a little imagination and a big dream." Former President of the United States Woodrow Wilson said:

> All big men are dreamers. They see things in the soft haze of a spring day or in the red fire of a long winter's evening. Some of us let our dreams die, but others nourish and protect them, nurse them through bad days till they bring them to sunshine and light, which always come to those who sincerely believe that their dreams will come true.

Somehow, when said like that, the idea of dreams doesn't sound so hokey anymore!

Nearly everything we see and experience in the world that comes from the efforts of our fellow humans is the result of what once began as only a dream. The paper you are holding in your hands, the light by which you read, and the furniture upon which you sit were all first conceived in the mind of a dreamer before they were brought to reality. That's the power of dreaming. It changes the world for the better.

One man who had a dream was William Lloyd Garrison. Born during the early 1800s, Garrison envisioned what must have seemed an impossible dream: abolishing slavery. According to author Walt Kallestad:

> Garrison dared to dream this in a day when slavery in the United States, in the North as well as the South, was

economically profitable and firmly entrenched. The influential governing body of one church declared that slavery was instituted by God. Key national figures insisted that the whole nation depended on slavery.

But Garrison had a dream. For over thirty years, he risked his life and fortune to publish an abolitionist newspaper called *The Liberator*. Among others, such as Frederick Douglass, Sojourner Truth, and Harriet Beecher Stowe, Garrison's voice for the abolition of slavery eventually turned the tide of popular opinion, and an impossible dream came true.

Walt Disney dreamed of creating a permanent carnival where children could play and their parents could be free of worry. The park would be safe, the sidewalks impeccably clean, and the fun creatively crafted to entertain people of all ages. He risked the entire fortune he'd amassed by drawing cartoon characters and went heavily into debt to see his dream launched. Disney not only created the world's most attended attractions, but he invented an entirely new form of entertainment: the modern-day theme park.

Dreams aren't fantasies or wishes. They aren't something for which someone hopes. Dreams are deep burning desires that drive the dreamer to create and accomplish and perform. W. Clement Stone said, "When you discover your mission, you will feel its demand. It will fill you with enthusiasm and a burning desire to get to work on it." That's the power of a dream; it grips you and won't let go. It drives you to step outside your comfort zone and reach for greatness. Dreams are special because they are sign posts to our destiny.

Getting a *Why*

There are many levels of dreams. There are dreams that are material or "surface level." There are others that are deeper and more meaningful. Still others transcend success and enter the realm of significance. Further still are the dreams that are concerned with personal destiny, God's purpose in our lives, and leaving a legacy. Whether a dream is big or small, shallow or deep, it is the effect it has on the dreamer that is important. To begin correctly, one must clearly identify a dream or multiple dreams that provide food for the soul. A dream grasps the attention of a person and won't let go. It dominates his or her thoughts and fuels his or her ambition. To neglect the power of dreams and their impact on our performance is to leave unused one of life's biggest levers.

To help you identify in as clear a fashion as possible those dreams that will motivate and drive you to perform, grab a pen and answer the following questions. Take your time. Have some fun. Dream a little! This step is easy, fun, and free. Even so, don't underestimate it. Don't rush past this section looking for the "specifics." To paraphrase Henry Ford, an expert on *how* always works for an expert on *why*. So start with *why*!

1. What would you do if you knew you couldn't fail? (In other words, what would you do if you were guaranteed to succeed?)
2. What would your life be like in five years if you could design it yourself? Answer this question in terms of several categories:

    a. Faith
    b. Family
    c. Finances
    d. Fitness
    e. Freedom
    f. Friends
    g. Following
    h. Fun

3. What did you enjoy doing as a child that you always wished you had pursued as an adult?
4. How do you want to be remembered? Write your epitaph as it would be if you died today. Now rewrite it as though you accomplished all your dreams.

Dreams

There are hundreds of questions that could be used to help clarify your dreams, but keeping the list to these four allows you a chance to deeply contemplate each one.

There is a haunting folk song written and performed by The Crash Test Dummies with the lyrics:

I'm still young, but I know my days are numbered
1234567 and so on
But a time will come when these numbers have all ended
And all I've ever seen will be forgotten

Our days are numbered. They are finite. It is important that we remember this. Moreover, not one of us knows the number of our days. It follows that we should therefore treat each day as a special gift from God. Sadly, though, we have each squandered time as though it had no value. We have each lived days, weeks, months, and perhaps even years as if we were going to live forever. Almost two millennia ago, the Roman Emperor Marcus Aurelius said, "Do not live as though you have a thousand years."

Renowned college football coach Lou Holtz, in his book *Winning Every Day,* tells the story of a student football player on his Notre Dame team named Alton Maiden. On a trip to Ireland, Maiden and the rest of the team made a sight-seeing trip to a twelfth-century monastery. While walking through the tiny grave-yard nearby, Maiden was inspired to write a poem called "The Dash," which concludes as follows:

After death has come and gone, a tombstone sits for
many to see.
But it serves no more than a symbol of a person's memory.
Under the person's name it reads the date of birth—and
the date the person passed.
But the more I think about the tombstone the only impor-
tant thing is the dash.
Yes, I see the name of the person, but that I might forget.
I also read the date of birth and death, but even that

5

might not stick.
But thinking about the person, I can't help but think to
remember the dash
Because it represents a person's life and that will
always last.
So when you begin to chart your life, make sure you are
on a positive path
Because people may forget your birth and death, but they
will never forget your dash.

We are all in our "dash" right now. What we do matters. What we do leaves a memory. As Gandalf the Grey says in the movie *The Lord of the Rings: The Fellowship of the Ring*, "All we have to decide is what to do with the time that is given to us." What you decide you want to do with the time given to you is your real dream.

LIFE Leadership is very flexible. Its rewards can be molded to fit the accomplishment of just about any dream someone may have. No matter how big or powerful someone's dream, success in LIFE Leadership can provide money and time and a network of relationships toward the fulfillment of that dream. But as powerful as the trends are and as effective as the LIFE Training Marketing System is, none of it works unless the LIFE Member has a clearly defined dream.

Dreams Aren't Fantasies

It is important at this point to warn you of something. Over our years in business, we have seen hundreds of people who could fill out a list of "the things they want." They can wax poetic about big houses, fancy cars, fabulous vacations, fine wardrobes, and time with family. They talk about buying an aircraft or racing cars. They speak of African safaris and trips to the moon. But when it comes to doing the work to earn these wonderful things, they sit on the couch and make excuses. These people are *not* dreamers; they are fantasizers. This is not what we mean by dreaming.

Making a fanciful list of all the wonderful things in which one is interested has a very small motivational effect. It is little more than materialism.

What we mean by dreaming is finding something that speaks to your inner core, something that whispers deeply to who you really are inside, something that resonates with the deepest fiber of your being. A real dream packs a wallop. It grabs a hold of you and won't let go. It is on your mind day and night. A real dream is something that you just have to accomplish. A real dream is something you are *supposed* to achieve. A dream or vision is tomorrow's reality expressed as an idea today.

Dreams Aren't Free

Dreams are precious. Dreams are powerful. But dreams aren't free. A real dream requires a price to be paid for its fulfillment. Once a dream is clearly defined, it is important to understand that commitment will be required to accomplish it. There will be no "something for nothing" when pursuing a true, God-given dream. As the saying goes, success is always on the other side of inconvenience.

These truths all apply to LIFE Leadership as well. There will be work involved. Commitments will be necessary. There will be new things to learn and do. Fulfilling a dream requires expanding the boundaries of your comfort zone.

Finally, it is important to understand that your commitment and work are not for a *business* but for your *dreams*. A business is just a vehicle that takes one to his or her dreams. We don't buy a car because we want to drive a car. We buy it because, first and foremost, we want it to take us somewhere. How much fun we have or how stylish we look or how fast we go getting there are just secondary considerations. So it is with LIFE Leadership; it is designed to get us to the accomplishment of our dreams. Along the way, we will certainly learn to enjoy the ride, but the key is that it gets us to our dreams. Effort is required, but it is worth it because our dreams are worth it!

Until you give yourself to some great cause, you haven't begun to fully live.
—John Mason

Every man dies; not every man really lives.
—Mel Gibson as William Wallace
in the movie *Braveheart*

Never let your fears stand in the way of your dreams.
—Unknown

Why not go out on a limb? Isn't that where the fruit is?
—Frank Sculley

Name: SANDY SPORTS
Quote: "Sounds great! I'll be ready to
        get going as soon as my
        softball league finishes up....
        oh, and my Tuesday night
        bowling league. Did I mention
        that I play beach volleyball
        every other weekend?"

CHAPTER 2

WEALTH THINKING
HOW YOU THINK DETERMINES HOW YOU LIVE

How we think is the most critical element in our success. How we see the world, how we interpret what we see, and what we decide based upon those interpretations is called *thinking*. As philosopher Francis Schaeffer explained, all our thoughts are skewed by something called our *worldview*. This is basically the lens through which we see and interpret all that is around us. To be successful financially requires proper wealth thinking, and this can only happen from a correct perspective or worldview.

As the ancient Greek philosopher Epictetus wrote in *Discourses*, "Appearances to the mind are of four kinds. Things either are what they appear to be; or they neither are, nor appear to be; or they are and do not appear to be; or they are not, and yet appear to be. Rightly to aim, in all these cases, is the wise man's task." Just trying to figure out what Epictetus is talking about is more thinking than most of us want to do! Maybe that's why Henry Ford said, "Thinking is the hardest work there is; that's why so few people engage in it." Hard work or not, thinking is *the* element in success.

Someone once asked, "Why do some people make it, while others quit?" The answer lies in their differences in thinking. LIFE Leadership is available to anybody of any stripe. The reason *everybody* doesn't make it is because some fail in their thinking. Their unsuccessful actions then follow their wrong thinking. This is perhaps the most important principle we have to teach in this entire book. The secret is to get your thinking right. Once that is accomplished, success can follow.

There are thoughts that are enablers of success, and there are their opposites: *disablers* of success. One might call this second category "limiting beliefs." It would be quite easy to list a bunch of beliefs that we commonly come across when talking to people about this industry. But it is much more productive, we think (no pun intended), to consider a list of *enabling* thoughts, or "empowering beliefs," which are actually worldview principles that will be required for success in any field—and certainly in building your community.

You Don't Know What You Don't Know

In order to develop proper thinking, it is important to have the attitude that we don't know everything already. If our finances are messed up, we don't have money figured out yet. If our relationships in life are messed up, we are not experts in dealing with people yet. The saying goes like this: *You don't know what you don't know*. We are the most ignorant about the things we are ignorant about. We don't even know that we don't know them. And this is precisely where we are hurt the most. Not knowing is what is holding us back. Further, much of what we know we are forgetting! And finally, many things we think we know may not even be so!

Therefore, we had better become students. We had better prepare to learn, to love learning, and to learn for the rest of our lives.

What does this have to do with thinking, you might ask? Everything! Thinking you know it all is a sure sign that no success will be coming your way. Thinking that you have a lot yet to learn is a sure sign that you can succeed and achieve even beyond where you are in life already. Proper thinking begins with a proper perspective on learning and wisdom. Returning once again to ancient Greece, it was said that Socrates was the wisest man of all. When asked why this might be so, he answered that if it were true, it was just because he was the only one in Athens who knew that he didn't know all the answers. There must be something to this. We're talking about him thousands of years later!

Success Can Be Learned

Once we realize that we don't know it all, the next conclusion ought to be that we can learn it all! "What?!" you might say.

One of the most enabling ways of thinking is to believe that if you don't know something, you *could* learn it if you wanted to badly enough. The fact that success can be learned is one of the most empowering beliefs a person can hold. While we certainly will never know it *all*, we can definitely learn what we need to succeed.

Tom Stoppard said, "Every ceiling, when reached, becomes a floor upon which one walks and now can see a new ceiling. Every exit is an entry somewhere." No matter where we are in life, we can move forward through learning. We like to use the analogy of water rushing along a ravine. It eddies and swirls violently and powerfully until it hits a dam. Then it presses up against the dam and settles to a rest. Unless the dam is removed, the water goes no further. Our education (and we're not only referring to the *formal* kind here) is a lot like that rushing water. When we learn something new, it is a breakthrough in our lives. We rush forward to success. But then, if we come to the edge of our learning, we are halted in our progress until the next lesson is learned. Then we are freed up for another breakthrough and go tumbling toward more success.

That is what learning does; it allows us to flow in the direction of our dreams. But none of this would happen, however, if we didn't first have the empowering thought that we *can* learn what we need to succeed. Without that belief, without that proper thinking, we are dead in the water (so to speak).

You Are Worthy of Success

Knowing that we don't know it all and believing that we can learn to succeed are not enough if we don't have a proper perspective about ourselves. It has been said that 95 percent of people have a low self-image, and the rest have a bad attitude. We don't know if that's true, but we have encountered scores of people who seem to think success is for "somebody else." This is destructive thinking of the highest order and is just not true. Success is a door that is open to all. Walking through it is what is required. It will never be easy; it will never be "overnight." But it will be worth it, and anybody can become worthy of it.

"But you don't know about me," someone might say.

"You don't understand my circumstances," another might reply.

"If you knew about my past, you'd never say I could still succeed."

"Success is not for people like me."

"I'm unlucky."

"I'm a victim."

We could continue this list for pages. But all of these replies (which we've actually heard many times) are lies. You can succeed. Yes, you. Everybody has had hard times. Everybody has had self-doubts. Everybody has regrets. Everybody has had bad breaks. But for every story of heartache, we can find someone somewhere who overcame much, much worse situations to achieve beyond most people's wildest dreams. It's all a matter of perspective. It's all a matter of *thinking*.

Believe you can, and you can. Believe you can't, and you can't. Either way, you are right. If you are prepared to learn what you need to learn and do what you need to do, you can succeed. Period.

Dreamers Are in the Minority

Something else to understand when you decide to chase after success is that you will be in the minority. Everybody loves the *idea* of success, but few ever truly pursue it. When you decide to step out beyond the crowd, be aware that the crowd does not like that. Proper thinking keeps this in perspective. Proper thinking dictates that being able to live in ways the common person cannot live will require doing things the common person will not do. Learn to become comfortable with being enthusiastic about something, even if those around you aren't.

Henry Wadsworth Longfellow said, "Not in the clamor of the crowded streets, not in the shouts or plaudits of the throng, but in ourselves are triumph and defeat." As author John Mason wrote, "More than anyone else, *you* must be persuaded." There is something singular about pursuing success. Comfort can be found in the crowd, but success is found in our individual dreams. Dreamers are a minority. Just like eagles, they are not found in flocks; they are found one at a time. Have the courage to stand on your own and stand for your dreams.

Criticism Is Normal for an Achiever

Courage is required because criticism accompanies all great achievement. As Albert Einstein said, "Great spirits have always encountered violent opposition from mediocre minds."

This is a new concept for many people. It was for us, too. When we followed the common success strategy taught to us by well-meaning individuals who were steeped in the philosophy of the out-of-date Industrial Age (which was to go to school, get good grades, and get a good, secure job with benefits), we received nothing but praise. But following that advice got us into debt and committed almost all of our waking hours to working jobs that weren't getting us anywhere. All the while, we were applauded and congratulated on being so "successful." Then we became entre-preneurs, and people lined up to tell us we were crazy. People who had never indicated any interest in our financial well-being before suddenly felt comfortable offering negative opinions about what we were doing! It seemed everybody had an opinion, and most of them were negative. Some were downright critical.

Dale Carnegie said, "Any fool can criticize, condemn, and complain, and most do." The way to understand criticism is to realize that all great achievement meets with resistance. In fact, attracting a few good critics can be a key indicator that you are on the road to success!

Here is what we eventually came to learn: People are free to say and think whatever they want. But *they* weren't the ones responsible for our lives and families or for paying our bills. It was up to us to decide what was best for our lives and to take the responsibility for our actions. That was one reason we worked and studied consistently to learn all we needed to learn to succeed—not that we know everything now. We have a long way to go, but our learning and efforts did pay off. We were able to leave our jobs and live the lifestyles we had dreamed of. And we did it in spite of the critics. John Mason said, "There's always a heavy demand for fresh mediocrity—don't give in to it."

As famous nineteenth-century author Edward Gibbon said, "I never make the mistake of arguing with people for whose opinions I have no respect." What we finally realized was that we should be seeking only the opinions of the people who had the results in life that we wanted to achieve ourselves. All other inputs were kindly ignored.

A Yiddish proverb says, "A critic is like the girl who can't dance so she says the band can't play." Don't worry about the criticism from those who can't dance. Focus instead on the music and don't miss your chance to dance!

Take the Long-Term View

Another form of proper, wealth thinking is to have a long-term view of things. Too many people in our society today want instant food, instant cash, instant coffee, and instant success. What we have learned is that the more you demand *now*, the less you can have *later*.

In *The Cashflow Quadrant*, author Robert Kiyosaki wrote:

There was a study done a number of years ago of rich and poor all around the world. The study wanted to find out how people born into poverty eventually become wealthy. The study found that these people...possessed three qualities. These qualities were:

1. They maintained a long-term vision and plan.
2. They believed in delayed gratification.
3. They used the power of compounding in their favor.

16

The study found that these people thought and planned for the long term and knew that they could ultimately achieve financial success by holding to a dream or a vision. They were willing to make short-term sacrifices to gain long-term success, the basis of delayed gratification.

Perhaps it is most impactful to consider the often-used demonstration of the penny doubling. The question is: Which appears to be more valuable: a million dollars paid in one lump sum or a penny on the first day added to double that amount on the second day, added to double that amount on the third day, and so on for just a month (we'll use thirty days)? Most of us have probably heard of this before, but it should never stop shocking us just how miraculously the penny doubling model adds up! Is it more than a million dollars? Way more! To be exact, it adds up to $10,737,418.23 (according to *The Math Forum @ Drexel*). No wonder Einstein famously quipped that compounding was the Eighth Wonder of the World! If money compounds this fabulously given the power of time and accumulation, imagine what human energy can accomplish if applied to similar long-term models of accumulation (such as in community building on the Internet)!

Notice the sub-point buried in all of this, too. How much money would you have on the first day? Just a penny. How much on the second day? Three cents. After five days, you'd only have thirty-one cents! But yet five days is one sixth of the entire time allotted! On the fifteenth day, *halfway into the allotted amount of time*, you'd have just $163.83! How many people get halfway into a worthy endeavor, only to give up because of "a lack of results" or "not enough progress"? As this model shows, such people are severely misguided, and it stems from their lack of a long-term view and their ignorance of the power of compounding.

There is another point here as well. Sometimes, people will get the idea that those building businesses in this industry are just in it for the money. To a certain extent, of course, that is true. Business is business, and one of the overriding purposes of a business is to generate income for its owner(s). So money is entirely acceptable as an appropriate measure of a business's performance. But the very concept of the power of compounding means that there must be a period of time where things are allowed to compound—meaning that there is a requirement for delayed gratification, that period of time in which there is little or no money rolling in. During this period, there must be other allurements and blessings to capture the affections of the business owner, long before the money shows up. This is one of the reasons LIFE Leadership has the motto: "Have Fun, Make Money, and Make a Difference."

In the early stages of business development, of course there is not going to be abundant wealth! Therefore, when one's first check is say, six dollars, he or she had better be having fun! And making a difference by serving and helping people can also happen immediately, long before money shows up, and along the entire journey as well. In our book *Launching a Leadership Revolution,* we introduced the concept of the "Trilateral Leadership Ledger," a concise way to measure one's personal, internal growth. As you build your business, you will become better in many areas of your life. You will be learning the principles of success along with the specifics of your business. You will be improving your people skills. You will be learning goal-setting and game-planning skills. These and many other aspects of personal growth along the journey are all blessings to be had that can and do come before the money does. All these things are important to keep in mind as one works to harvest the fruits of delayed gratification and the power of compounding.

Proper wealth thinking always requires the long-term view of things. All good things take time. Delayed gratification and a mature expectation of the time required to obtain results are critical to accomplishing meaningful, lasting success. As President James Garfield said, "When God wants to grow a squash, He grows it in one summer; but when He wants to grow an oak, He takes a century."

Big Things Come from Little Things

One of the most successful athletic coaches of all time is Coach John Wooden. The summary of his achievements while head coach of the UCLA Bruins basketball team is staggering:

- Ten national championships (a record)
- Seven national championships in a row (a record)
- Eighty-eight consecutive victories (a record)
- Thirty-eight straight tournament playoff wins (a record)
- Four perfect seasons (a record)
- Only one losing year—his first—in forty-one years of coaching!

His formula for success is both simple and surprising. One of his biggest precepts is the concept that "little things make big things happen." Wooden says, "Often we place such emphasis on distant goals that inadequate attention is given to what it takes to get there. To me, this is less about being a perfectionist and more about having a determination to be seeking improvement constantly. Success, not the devil, is in the details." Wooden maintains that there is a correct and most effective way to do everything. When coaching the UCLA Bruins, Wooden said, "I was not trying to create robots that simply did as they were told, but rather individuals who were *extremely* well grounded in the correct fundamentals, who had good performance habits. Little things, done well, make big things happen."

Understanding this simple but profound philosophy is crucial for building a community with LIFE Leadership. This book is crammed full of details and fundamentals that, if mastered, can lead to enormous success. But to do that, they must be *mastered*. Doing enough of the right things in the right way for a long enough period of time is what produces success.

Take Responsibility

A famous saying states: "If it's to be, it's up to me." While the LIFE Training Marketing System is distinguished for its ability to help people build teams of people and its specialty of developing *communities* of people through which informational products and services flow, it might seem surprising to say, "If it's to be, it's up to me." But that is exactly where success must start. In fact, most achievement is team or group achievement. Anything worthwhile in our lives involves other people. But the greatest explosion begins with a tiny spark. To build a team first requires the spark of an individual.

Taking personal responsibility for one's actions *and* the results of those actions is not an option for anyone desiring a successful life. British Prime Minister, Home Secretary, First Lord of the Admiralty, Chancellor of the Exchequer, and perhaps the greatest Englishman who ever lived Winston Churchill said, "However tempting it might be to some, when much trouble lies ahead, to step aside adroitly and put someone else up to take the blows, I do not intend to take that cowardly course, but, on the contrary, to stand up to my post and persevere according to my duty." Churchill's example is one of proper thinking. Applied to a business owner's life, it will be an example of wealth thinking also. The wealth in life finds its way into the hands of those who assume the most responsibility for their actions.

Focus Only on What You Can Control

Having a good attitude is another paramount principle of correct thinking. A good attitude results from a proper perspective. And a proper perspective leads us to work within our sphere of influence and leave the rest aside. The Bible says, "Take therefore no thought for the morrow: for the morrow shall take thought for the things of itself. Sufficient unto the day is the evil thereof" (Matthew 6:34, KJV). Another way to say this is to focus only on what you can control.

While we have just surveyed the importance of taking personal responsibility, we should guard against the tendency to assume responsibility for too much. What do we mean by too much? We mean things that are outside our area of influence. If something is beyond our ability to affect it, it should not have the ability to worry us. John Lubbock said, "A day of worry is more exhausting than a day of work." The most effective business owners are the ones who focus on what they can directly control and leave all other things to the side. This keeps things simple and allows the business owners to focus on the steps they can take to bring about the desired future. Getting caught up in little things or circumstances is a destructive, distracting activity that leads to mediocrity. Focusing only on what is important and under our immediate control is one of the golden strategies of wealth.

It's Not What Happens; It's How You Handle It

Another key aspect to having a good attitude is to realize that, as Stephen Covey says, "Between stimulus and response, we have a choice." We can choose how to respond. We like to say, "It's not what happens to you; it's how you respond that counts."

We *will* all have troubles and struggles. After all, problems are the price of success. The most successful people are the ones who respond maturely and appropriately to the challenges that come along. First, they analyze those problems in terms of the bigger picture. This brings a proper perspective as we discussed above. Next, they determine the most productive course of action instead of the natural, emotional one. Third, they take appropriate action with a good attitude. And finally, they monitor the results and learn from them. This is all very easy to write about and to discuss in theory, but it is infinitely more difficult to put into practice in our lives. However, those who learn to think this way truly develop wealth thinking and the positive results that go along with it.

Excuses Are Useless, Except for Preventing Success

One thing you will never see is a champion who makes excuses. The two concepts simply cannot coexist. According to Willis Whitney, "Some men have thousands of reasons why they cannot do what they want to do when all they really need is one reason why they can." And George Washington Carver said, "Ninety-nine percent of failures come from people who have a habit of making excuses."

When a loser fails, he or she places blame or makes excuses. When a winner fails, he or she takes personal responsibility and admits his or her failings. In fact, it has been said that one is not a failure until he or she blames someone else or makes an excuse. Nursing pioneer Florence Nightingale said, "I attribute my success to this: I never gave or took an excuse." As the saying goes, "If you really want to do something, you'll find a way; if you don't, you'll find an excuse." Or perhaps it is better stated, "If you don't want to do something, nobody can stop you!"

Commit to Your Dreams

The final aspect we'll consider in this section on wealth thinking is commitment. Many people begin the journey of success in life, but few finish well. In fact, one commentator said there were four hundred leaders mentioned as influential in the Bible, but only about eighty of these "finished strong." Why is that? The answer is: a lack of commitment.

Author Joe Griffith said:

> You cannot keep a committed person from success. Place stumbling blocks in his way, and he takes them for stepping-stones, and on them he will climb to greatness. Take away his money, and he makes spurs of his poverty to urge him on. The person who succeeds has a program; he fixes his course and adheres to it; he lays his plans and executes them; he goes straight to his goal. He is not pushed this side and that every time a difficulty is thrust in his way. If he can't go over it, he goes through it.

Any significant achievement requires a healthy dose of commitment. Football legend Vince Lombardi said, "There is only one way to succeed in anything and that is to give everything. I do and I demand that my players do. Any man's finest hour is when he has worked his heart out in a good cause and lies exhausted on the field of battle...victorious." That's commitment, and commitment produces another result: tenacity. As Lombardi also said, "The harder you work, the harder it is to surrender."

Whether you think you can, or you think
you can't—you're right.
—Henry Ford

Enough experience will make you wise.
—James R. Cook

It is better to be wise than to seem wise.
—Origen (c. 185-254 A.D.)

Isn't it splendid to think of all the things
there are to find out about?
—Lucy Montgomery

Name: SELFISH SAM

Quote: "So how much can I make? Really?! Is there some way we can set it up so my wife can't get any of it?"

CHAPTER 3

THE NEXT STEP PROGRAM
BECOMING A
PROFESSIONAL BUSINESS OWNER

Having a burning desire or dream is the most important step toward success. But once you've clearly established what you want and have begun the journey of learning the correct thinking, it's time for action. With LIFE Leadership, we each have an opportunity equally matched to our dreams, and we have something we can "do" to make those dreams come true.

Stretches and Warm-Ups

An athlete showing up to training camp starts with some basic orientation, followed by stretches and warm-ups. If you are brand new to LIFE Leadership, there are a couple of early activities we highly recommend to get yourself acclimated. Consider them to be stretches and warm-ups.

First and foremost, review the "LIFE Leadership Member Compensation Plan and Income Disclosure Statement" brochure. And as soon as possible, attend an Open Meeting in your area (or a webcast version of the event) and the next seminar that becomes available. (Note: If you have already purchased your business starter kit, in it you received access to four weekly Open Meetings as well as access for two to the next available Monthly Seminar. Simply give your LIFE Member number at the door to gain entry.) We also recommend, if you haven't already, that you review the materials in the *First Night Pack*. These are the most important steps to take to begin understanding what you've got your hands on.

Training Camp

During the period of attending your first meetings and reviewing these initial materials, it may be helpful to consider this as your "training camp." The purpose of training camp is to get new participants up to speed with the details of being on the team and to get them in shape for the season ahead. Ultimately, in sports, when rookies come to training camp, it is for the purpose of being fashioned into professionals.

We have a similar approach. It is called the Next Step Program, and it is designed to help new LIFE Members become Professional Business Owners (PBOs). (For specific details about the Next Step Program, please consult "The Next Step Program" brochure or the free PDF download on lifeleadership.com.) The four steps comprising the Next Step Program are as follows:

These four steps become the foundation upon which you attract customers for your business and build a community of people who do the same. Simply sign in to lifeleadership.com and click on each step in order to advance, or fill out "The Next Step Program" brochure and hand it to your upline support team for processing.

Resting on this foundation, then, are the sequences of accomplishment that will take you upward toward "living the life you've always wanted." It may be best to envision this process as a ladder of successive rungs of accomplishment.

The Next Step Program

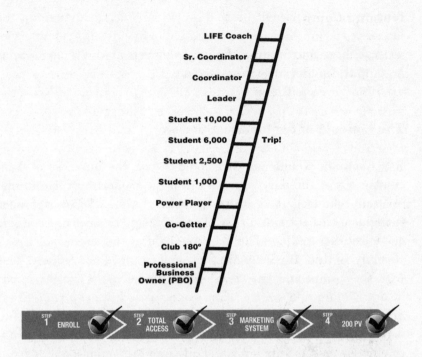

Once you have set yourself up as a Professional Business Owner by taking the four steps in the Next Step Program, you have reached the first rung on the ladder. The next one is called Club 180°, which is a simple game designed to develop the productive habits of listening to audios and contacting prospects about your products and your business. It is simply a fun way to track your daily activity. (For details about Club 180°, download the free PDF at lifeleadership.com/DesktopModules/Life_Forms/Forms/LIFE_Club_180_V3.pdf.)

The next rung on the ladder is Go-Getter, which is what we call anyone who shows fifteen or more product sales approaches or business plans in a month. The rung after that is Power Player, which is our dominant "play" for building your business big! (More about this later).

These first four rungs on the ladder, *PBO*, *Club 180°*, *Go-Getter*, and *Power Player*, are steps that you will maintain throughout your career with LIFE Leadership. In other words, you will continue taking them again and again. In fact, mastering these four, easy, fundamental steps will be the key to advancing further up the ladder to the life you've always wanted to live! It's that simple: Get good at these four basics. And use them repeatedly to advance as high up the ladder of success as you wish!

It's all systematic.

The Concept of Systematic Success

Ray Kroc, the founder of McDonald's, took the business of franchising out of the dark ages and into the modern era. He fundamentally changed it in order to make it work. What was once thought to be a scam and possibly even illegal has become a staple of American retailing. The principle behind the success of Kroc's strategy is this: Business runs on ability and knowledge. Those with the ability and knowledge have the success. Those without it, don't, plain and simple. Kroc systematized the *sharing* of best practices and business wisdom *from* the successful *to* the hopeful. A new business owner could know nothing about business, franchising, or restaurants but could buy into McDonald's and learn it all. As the restaurant owner grew his business and prospered, so too would the parent company for sharing its expertise.

Ray Kroc bought something called the "McDonald's system" from the founding McDonald brothers in California. Their system was a finely detailed method of operating their store that was proven to bring profits. Success was not left to chance; it was systematized. This system is readily apparent when simply walking into a McDonald's restaurant. The menu is above the counter, the fry machine is to the left, the bathrooms are to the right, and the children's play area is right out front. And these are just the obvious details. Bookkeeping, inventory management, staffing, and inspections are all regimented and systematic. The McDonald's system works so well that nearly every restaurant in North America makes money each year!

In LIFE Leadership, we have no restaurant or facility. We have no inventory or cleanliness inspections. We have no playground. But we *do* have proven best practices that work in our industry. We *do* have a systematic, proven approach to success.

The Play

That systematic approach is called the Power Player Program, designed so that LIFE Members will experience consistent growth. **Power Players embody the ultimate business-building characteristics.** Steve Sabol of NFL Films said, "Good players turn up at the right time or the right place, or do the right things. Great players do all three." In LIFE Leadership, the "great" players are the Power Players. Power Players learn the right things, apply them properly, and focus on and achieve the right results.

We love sports. Athletic competitions embody the success principles that are required to succeed in life in nearly any field. Sports represent the classic struggles of man against man, army against army, and man against himself. We must confess football is a favorite. We like the contact, the strategy, and the heroic catches and last-second finishes.

Imagine a football team that can't be stopped: a team with an offensive play that scores every time. The players break huddle and get into position along the line of scrimmage. The quarterback barks out the signals, and the center snaps the ball. All the blocking works perfectly, and the play scores *every time*! Can you even imagine such a thing?

With LIFE Leadership, there is actually such a play. The LIFE Member goes up to the line and barks out the play, "Power Player!" Everybody knows it is the play that will be called. It is the same play he called on the previous drive. It's the same play he called in last week's game and all of last season. But it scores every time! It has never been stopped.

Power Player is an all-encompassing business-building program with a proven track record. In fact, it has worked so well year after year that we keep on calling the same play over and over. Those who use it and execute it properly have growing businesses, repeatedly and predictably.

The point is that growth becomes predictable. It is not a question of whether it works. It is a question of whether you work it. If you follow the proven pattern, if you call the Power Player play, if you stay consistent, the results are extremely predictable.

Please notice that we didn't say it was easy. We didn't say it was something for nothing. We didn't say it was guaranteed—because nothing in life is. But it is reasonably *predictable*. You can expect reasonable results for the right amount of consistent, correct inputs. Continue those inputs according to the Power Player strategy, and the results crescendo and grow to larger and larger levels. Soon, what you once thought of as "good money" doesn't seem so good any more. What you once thought of as a "good job" might not seem so good anymore. Gradually and consistently, you will be growing in financial ability and will start "checking off" dreams along the way. All this and more can happen because of a little concept called Power Player.

The Program

The Power Player Program is broken down into three main areas:

1. Theory
2. Activity
3. Results

Theory is important because *you don't know what you don't know*. And this is particularly true when it comes to this profession. One may be a successful professional, a small business owner or a teacher; one may have succeeded financially before or have obtained a top-notch education, but that doesn't make that person an expert here. This is a whole new ball game. Certainly the life skills obtained in other occupations, such as people skills, goal setting, and continuing education, can be useful in building a community in LIFE Leadership. But there is a specific body of material that must be mastered in order for a LIFE Member to know what to do, how to do it, and how to duplicate it. One of the best ways to learn is through experience—that is, experience of those who have been successful. That's what the theory part of the program provides.

Activity is critical because all the theory in the world is useless unless it is applied to something. Learning should not lead to knowledge; rather, it should lead to action.

Finally, a focus on *results* is paramount because without working toward something specific and without following an exact strategy, a business owner can learn a lot and do a lot but still not accomplish a lot. Success is not knowledge. Success is not being busy. Success is getting results.

The Power Player Program embodies all three of these areas and breaks them down into manageable parts. The chapters to follow will explore each of these areas (theory, activity, and results) more closely.

The most beautiful thing in the world is, precisely, the conjunction of learning and inspiration.
—Wanda Landowska

It's not how much time you put into something that counts. It's what you put into the time that counts.
—Unknown

We can't take any credit for our talents. It's how we use them that counts.
—Madeleine L'Engle

When you convert ideas into action, you are seldom disappointed.
—Alexander Lockhart

A man is not old until his regrets take the place of his dreams.
—John Barrymore

Name: SUSIE STATUS
Quote: "Are there any famous
          people in this? We have a
          reputation in this
          community, and I'm not
          sure we could tell our
          friends about this unless
          there are famous people
          involved."

CHAPTER 4

THEORY

READ, LISTEN, AND ASSOCIATE

The best way to begin in business is with a good attitude, and the most important attitude to have is that of a *student*. Many people start with a critical eye; they pass judgment on everything they are told and everything that takes place and think they know how and what they should be taught to succeed. But as our friend and business partner Tim Marks says, "This business doesn't necessarily build the way you might think it does." Therefore, begin your journey as a *student* and not as a *critic*.

Learning is one of life's biggest blessings. It can and should be fun and rewarding. These truths are more relevant when the learning is in an area about which the individual is enthusiastic. The more excited one is about building his or her business, the more fun and the faster the learning will be. Realize that successful people are hungry learners. In our book *Launching a Leadership Revolution*, we dedicated a whole chapter to the concept of learning as the first step on the stairway to leadership greatness. This is because without the attitude of a student and without the understanding that there is always something more to learn, an individual will be limited in his or her accomplishments. One never arrives. One never gets to the place where he or she has it "all figured out." There is *always* more to learn.

Another important component of success is learning from those who have succeeded themselves. Everybody has an opinion; all that's required is a mouth that works! But that doesn't mean those opinions have any validity when it comes to personal achievement. As we said before, *success begins with information from the correct source.* In other words, be careful from whom you learn; they might not have the results you want! If you listen to broke people about finances, chances are you'll pick up their habits and end up with their financial situation. If you listen to the wealthy, your chances of success skyrocket.

The Power Player Program organizes the learning that is required to build a community by imparting both principles and specifics from those who have succeeded. The program is designed to fit the lifestyles of most people who are too busy to attend classroom instruction and can't afford expensive tuitions, and it follows the pattern of learning recommended by so many of the world's most successful. As coauthor of the wildly popular *Chicken Soup for the Soul* series, Mark Victor Hansen says, "Read books, listen to tapes, and attend seminars—they are decades of wisdom reduced to invaluable hours." Additionally, the learning associated with the Power Player Program is affordable and flexible to fit in your schedule.

The educational steps involved in the theory portion of the Power Player Program are:

1. Subscribe to the LIFE Training Marketing System.
2. Purchase and listen to the *Top 50 CD Pack*.
3. Attend Open Meetings and Night Owls (LIFE Library).
4. Attend Monthly Seminars (LIFE Live).
5. Attend Leadership Conventions ("Major Functions").

To be recognized as a Power Player, each of the theory items of the program must be fulfilled (as well as the aspects of the activity and results categories to be explained in subsequent chapters). Again, a Power Player is a big accomplishment. Someone who has achieved Power Player joins an inner circle of performers. Power Players receive special recognition, have special meetings and training focuses, and are provided special seating at the Leadership Conventions. Don't panic if you don't think you can do all of these steps right away. Just work toward them and know the rewards for Power Player will be well worth it, in many ways!

LIFE Training Marketing System

A wealth of information can be gained through what might be called "passive learning." This is learning that takes place easily while one is doing something else, such as driving to work or completing chores. Audio recordings are one of the best sources of passive learning. Author Brian Tracy said that if one listens to experts in a given field for thirty minutes a day, that person will be as informed as anyone on the topic in just a year and an expert within another year. We have no way to verify the timeline of this claim, but we know it to be true in spirit. That's because it worked for us. We were both in poor financial condition when someone introduced us to an audio training program. Without that training, we would not be where we are today. Period—without a doubt!

Audio recordings are an extremely convenient, portable source of education. In the LIFE Training Marketing System, the audios are recordings of speeches or training sessions given by leaders worldwide. Each speaker featured on an audio recording has attained a leadership level and has proven his or her ability to grow a community. This is where the value of the audios comes in: the information contained therein.

"I can buy blank CDs at the store for forty cents," someone might say.

"Yes," we could reply, "but listening to them will produce no financial results in your life. They are blank! It's not the CD itself but the information that is important." It's the information that makes the audios so valuable. And it is information with a proven track record.

The audios that come with the Marketing System subscription are designed to build expertise on the part of a business owner consistently over a period of time. The periodical nature of the audios that come each month through the Marketing System has proven to be critical. This is for several very important reasons. First, most people do not join LIFE Leadership with what could be called wealth thinking, as we've already discussed. (Even in the remote cases where someone has experienced personal financial success, it is still necessary to obtain specifics.) We need to be "de-educated" on all the incorrect things we have learned over the years about money, success, and accomplishment. Second, we receive a large amount of friction, negative input, and abrasion on a *daily* basis, whether in the workforce, at home, or around friends and family. So there is a combined need to "undo" all the cumulative wrong that has been programmed into our brains and also to combat the new negative on an ongoing basis. For these reasons, like an antibiotic fighting off a germ, the audio recordings provide a consistent dosage. There is also an entertainment factor to the audios that is hard to quantify. They are fun to listen to! Most people find they have a better attitude when regularly listening to LIFE Training audios. After all, it's just good food for the soul to hear positive, uplifting, and encouraging words in a world normally full of cynicism and hurt.

But the audio portion of the LIFE Training Marketing System is one small part of the package. In addition to the eight audios provided each month, subscribers also get access to the LIFE Training channel on Rascal Radio. If you are not yet familiar, Rascal Radio is an online and/or mobile radio station that you can customize to your listening pleasure. Filled with all of the LIFE Training audios produced since we launched the company, you can program a channel featuring your favorite speaker, combine that with a favorite topic, and listen to randomly selected recordings. You can also mark favorites, skip ahead, rate the recordings, and even purchase one on the spot if you'd like to retain your own copy. Many LIFE Members utilize Rascal Radio for a large part of their audio training because it is so portable, can be Bluetoothed to play in their car, etc. It provides all the benefits of the audio training habit described above in a portable or online platform.

One final piece of the educational aspect of the Marketing System is the Video Library, featuring hundreds of videos by LIFE Leadership's top business builders and trainers. Listening to audios is one thing, but watching videos can offer learning in visual ways that audio cannot. With the Marketing System, you get both in abundance.

The remaining pieces of the Marketing System are geared toward helping you attract and retain retail customers, such as the Branded Email skins, the Personal Home Pages, the "Share Your LIFE" online presentation tool (for showing the marketing plan to someone at a distance), and the LIFE Line smartphone app communication tool. All of these benefits, both educational and operational, are all rolled into one easy-to-obtain Marketing System.

All Power Players are involved with the LIFE Training Marketing System.

Top 50 CD Pack

Throughout the years, LIFE Training has produced numerous recordings that have gained widespread popularity among business owners for their teaching content, specific strategies, principles, or sheer motivational value. The *Top 50 CD Pack* is a compilation of the best of the best recordings produced in our history. And let us tell you, it is not an easy list to assemble! Narrowing down the vast list of recordings to just fifty is nearly impossible. Discussion about which audios make it into the list can go on for hours and hours, with input from top leaders throughout the continent fighting it out and calling each other names! Okay, not really. But there is a lot of wringing of hands and gnashing of teeth—not a pretty sight. So you can imagine the potency of the audios that are left standing after all of this! These are the absolute best LIFE Training has to offer a business owner about building his or her business.

The *Top 50 CD Pack* used to come in a black box. The intent was, and still is, for this pack to serve as a LIFE Member's personal library on success. Its information is indestructible, just like the black box recorders used in commercial airliners. When a plane crashes, the black box is always recovered in working order (which makes one wonder why they don't make the entire plane out of that black box material). These audios should be listened to again and again. It has been said that the better a LIFE Member knows his Top 50, the better he knows his business.

There have been examples where people have begun a business at a distance from any other significant LIFE Leadership activity and had access to information primarily through the *Top 50 CD Pack*. Armed solely with this, they were able to build their business successfully. That is because this one pack encompasses so much information!

Power Players own their own *Top 50 CD Pack*, and they learn from it continually.

Open Meetings (LIFE Library)

One of the most critical components in building a community is Open Meetings (either live or via webcast). Open Meetings, or simply "Opens," as they are often called, are actually not open. Rather, they are invitation-only affairs. However, they are open to any LIFE Member and guests he or she cares to bring along.

The primary purpose of Open Meetings is to provide an introductory environment for new people to check out LIFE Leadership. The first part of the meeting concentrates on "showing the plan" (described in depth in chapter six). Here, the LIFE Leadership products and compensation plan are presented by one of the top leaders in the business. This can be considered the "what it is" part of the meeting. The second part of the meeting, called the "Night Owl," focuses on teaching new or prospective LIFE Members how to actually begin building the business for themselves. This can be considered the "how to do it" part of the meeting.

Attending Open Meetings is important for several reasons. First, Opens are intended to introduce new people to the business. LIFE Leadership sponsors these meetings as a tool for people to use in building their LIFE Leadership community. As a LIFE Member exposes new people to the concept, the Open Meetings are there to give prospects a second look. Next, Opens provide the Members in attendance a picture of the proper way to present their business, or to "show the plan." One of the best ways to learn is through exposure and repetition. Week after week, as Members see the plan drawn out by different leaders, they increase their own ability to explain the program. Third, Open Meetings are a chance for Members to associate with their team and upline and develop the relationships that are key to building communities for the long term. Fourth, the "Night Owl," or second portion of the meeting, focuses mainly on the what, why, and how of becoming a Power Player. So Opens are a main source of training for Members that want their business to grow fast and profitably. Fifth, Open Meetings are very exciting. They are an excellent source of motivation and can help keep LIFE Members focused and consistent, much as the LIFE Training Marketing System does. Some Members have said they can't wait for Tuesday night (when most Open Meetings are conducted) to roll around so they can get their weekly dose of positiveness in an otherwise negative world.

Power Players subscribe to access to the Open Meetings through a program called the LIFE Library. It is so named because it comes automatically with an enormous video library featuring all of LIFE Leadership's top speakers and authors teaching life-changing information. Subscribing to the LIFE Library is also a convenience for LIFE Members because it provides electronic access to all Open Meetings in their market. All LIFE Members need do to gain access is show their LIFE Member number upon entry. As an extra benefit, all LIFE Members who subscribe to the LIFE Library receive some bonus PV (point value) each month for doing so.

Power Players attend all weekly Open Meetings and Night Owls, and they do so by subscribing to the LIFE Library.

Monthly Seminars (LIFE Live)

Seminars are held monthly at locations around the world and can vary in size from a couple hundred attendees to thousands upon thousands, depending on the area. The LIFE Training seminar system is designed to teach the what, why, and how of building communities in LIFE Leadership. This training picks up where the weekly Night Owls leave off. The teaching is both expository (explained) and demonstrative (through personal stories) and, therefore, reaches across all varieties of learning styles in the audience. Ask any successful community builder, and he or she will say that the seminars have been critical to his or her success. Seminars are also an excellent opportunity to recognize achievers for their performance in the preceding month, and this is done for varying levels throughout the event.

These events are ticketed in advance, much like a sporting event—but much more valuable to the attendee! For the convenience of LIFE Members, LIFE Live enables people to subscribe to access to these meetings so they never miss an event. As a bonus, there is extra PV (point value) given each month to all LIFE Live subscribers. In this program, subscribers merely show their LIFE Member number at the door for access. (Of course, nonsubscribers can buy a single ticket or pay at the door). Power Players are LIFE Live subscribers because it helps them build their business faster! And all Power Players, of course, attend the Monthly Seminars.

Leadership Conventions ("Major Functions")

Leadership Conventions are the granddaddy of the entire LIFE Training system. They are the crème de la crème, the cake under the icing, the iceberg under the tip, the ponies under the hood, the—you get the idea. Leadership Conventions (often referred to as "Major Functions" or even just "Majors") are continental conventions that provide the chance for business owners throughout a large geographic region to gather and learn from LIFE Leadership's best trainers. At these conventions, sales competition winners are recognized, top sales teams are announced, high-level recognition is showcased, business building competition winners are awarded, and an overall arrangement of topics and speakers comprising information from every aspect of building a community business are presented. Leadership Conventions are the culmination of months of business growth through the local Open Meetings and Monthly Seminars. These events comprise three days worth of training and even offer special meetings available only to Power Players or other high-level achievers.

For many reasons, Leadership Conventions are the most important events of the year. Nearly every leader within LIFE

Leadership can trace his or her decision to build his or her business back to something that was said or happened at a Leadership Convention. As is commonly claimed, "life-altering decisions are made at Leadership Conventions." One of the reasons for this is that LIFE Members tend to get the "big picture" at Leadership Conventions. The experience might be analogous to attending a live concert versus listening to a recording of the same artist. There is just something magical about being on location with all our senses taking in everything that happens. The amount of information and perspective conveyed is so comprehensive, in fact, nearly overwhelming, that people understand just how big this industry is and where it is heading. That understanding leads to belief. Belief leads to results, and that's the reason to attend in the first place—to obtain results!

Power Players attend the Leadership Conventions because they generate results like no other event!

* * *

The purpose of the LIFE Training meetings just discussed (Open Meetings, Monthly Seminars, and Leadership Conventions) is to provide association with successful people. To paraphrase author Robert Kiyosaki, our income will probably be somewhere in the ballpark of the people we hang around the most often. More important, we have discovered that the best experience is *somebody else's*. These various meetings provide the opportunity to associate with those who have experience and success that we can utilize in order to shorten our journey and increase our wealth thinking. For most of us, finding someone who is financially successful and who is willing to teach us how he or she accomplished it is nearly impossible. If we *do* happen to know somebody who has succeeded to the financial levels we desire for ourselves, he or she usually has no compelling reason to share that experience with us. The meetings of the LIFE Training Marketing System formalize that association and sharing of experience to the benefit of all who attend. As Kiyosaki stated in *The Business School*:

One of the beauties of [community building businesses] is that [they give] you the opportunity to face your fears, deal with your fears, overcome your fears, and let the winner in you win. To me, learning to sell, learning to overcome my fear of rejection, and learning to get my point across is the best education I have ever received.

The LIFE Training system (especially its meetings) provides just that kind of education and environment.

Summary

Power Players are not afraid of learning; as a matter of fact, they crave it. Power Players plug into the full line of training aids to maximize their learning and grow their effectiveness. They know that learning by listening and reading and then associating with others that have succeeded through the various meetings available is their fastest path to success.

Theory is required to help LIFE Members avoid the time-wasting process of trial and error. The fastest and safest path to success is in the footsteps of those who have already succeeded. The LIFE Training Marketing System embodied by the Power Player Program provides just that: the path of knowledge to the place where dreams can come true.

Alas, there is no something for nothing. Knowledge and learning alone will not generate success. Although LIFE Training provides a pathway of knowledge, that pathway must still be traversed. That brings us to the next section: activity.

It's what you learn after you know it all that counts.
—John Wooden

What is defeat? Nothing but education; nothing but the first step to something better.
—Wendell Phillips

The unexamined life is not worth living.
—Plato

The next best thing to being clever is being able to quote someone who is.
—Mary Pettibone Poole

Only the educated are free.
—Epictetus

The only real ill-doing is the deprivation of knowledge.
—Plato

Name: BETTY BUSY-BODY
Quote: "Huh? Oh, go ahead. I'm listening. You don't mind if I take care of a few things while you talk, do you?"

CHAPTER 5

ACTIVITY, PART ONE
MAKING THE LIST AND CONTACTING

Action is the handle that turns the crank on the machinery of theory—because sooner or later work is required to make one's dreams come true. An anonymous quote states: "The superior man is modest in his speech but superior in his *actions*."

There are several parts involved in the activity portion of building a community of people through which life-changing information flows. It is important to understand right up front that none of these are difficult in and of themselves. Each involves basic activities we have all done throughout our lives. Applying these basic functions to LIFE Leadership is what will be *new* to the beginning LIFE Member, *new* but not *difficult*. This is truly one of the most exciting things about LIFE Leadership: the fact that anybody can do it. It doesn't require a certain education or background; one doesn't have to be "cerebral" or have experience in sales, and it doesn't involve learning to do things that only certain people have the talent to accomplish. The basic steps involved are achievable by *anyone*. Truly, anyone can build LIFE Leadership. It simply takes a decision to do the work.

It sometimes seems as though there is a "culture of complacency" in our society today. Somehow it has become acceptable to be average. Mediocrity is presented as "cool." Dissidence is presented as "artistic." But these are lies. They always have been, and they always will be.

Someone once asked us if the perils afflicting our society were due to ignorance or apathy. Our answer was that we didn't know, and we didn't care!

Okay, we'll get serious.

Achievement, effort, personal growth, work, and pursuit of excellence are virtues; their opposites are *not*. There should be no shame in hard work; in fact, hard work should be a source of pride. By pride, we don't mean the wrong kind of pride where one puts himself ahead of others and becomes boastful. We mean the self-satisfaction of knowing that you have given your very best to something, that indeed, you have tried your hardest. Think about it. When was the last time you *really* tried your *hardest* at something? Does your current job or profession require you to be *excellent*? Or can you just "get by"? Our bet is that many simply get by. In fact, there is a humorous saying that rings a little too true: "Companies will pay just enough to keep people from quitting, while people will do just enough to keep from getting fired." It doesn't have to be that way. Where true reward is available, true effort can be expended. That's what LIFE Leadership is all about: helping people get rewarded for performance. What LIFE Leadership stands for, and what will be required to accomplish a dream lifestyle, is individuals or couples committed to accepting a challenge and giving it their best. Half-throttle efforts produce half-throttle lifestyles—or less. But real effort brings immeasurable rewards.

The activity of building this type of business consists of effort in two main areas:

1. Generating Product Flow
2. Building a Community

In one way or another, this entire book deals with generating product flow (which will also be covered in chapter nine) and building a community.

Building a community is the key task every great company must learn to achieve in order to have a loyal, continuing customer base. As we described earlier, Dell Computer Corporation founder Michael Dell emphasized that developing a community of loyal, repeat buyers online is the key skill in today's new economy. It is this unique ability that LIFE Leadership teaches and supports. And it is this unique ability that sets us apart from the rest.

The Five-Step Pattern

Accomplishing the building of such a community, then, is of the utmost importance. It is done using the Five-Step Pattern (sometimes called "The Loop"), which involves:

1. Generating a List of Names
2. Contacting
3. Showing the Plan
4. Following Through
5. Getting Them Started (Rotating the Pattern)

As discussed above, these steps are very straightforward and simple to do. They involve activity anyone can do. Still, there are specifics to learn about each that will make the business owner the most effective. Remember, following proven patterns is a legitimate shortcut to success.

Generating a List of Names

Step number one in the Five-Step Pattern is making a list of names. This seems almost too elementary to warrant discussion. After all, who hasn't made a list before—of groceries, tasks, or whatever? Believe it or not, there are a few things to know in this step. There are some best practices that have proven to work very effectively.

The beginning LIFE Member is encouraged to obtain a copy of the brochure "Who Do You Know?" and to reference the "How to Get Started" materials.

The first thing to know about making a list of names of potential individuals to contact is that this first step is a brainstorming exercise. The intent is to empty the brain entirely of every contact you have ever known. This doesn't mean you think they would all be good at the business or that you know how to get in touch with them. All you are trying to accomplish is a flow of names. By not prejudging any name that comes to mind, you free your brain to think of the next one. Hold nothing back. Have fun with it and see how large you can make your initial list. Many times, you may only remember a first name or sometimes even less. You may simply know one as "the man who works at the accounting office." That's fine. Just find some way to record your recognition of that person and move on. The goal is to write down as many names as possible. All sorting and guessing who would be most likely to respond positively to the business idea can come later.

The second thing to know about making a list of names is that it should be written. We have seen many, many people get started in this industry and attempt to build it by keeping their names "in their head." Read carefully: *That doesn't work*! Feel free to verify it if you want, but you can save a lot of time by writing down a list of names from the very beginning of your business. "Why?" you might ask. We'll illustrate with a recurring story from LIFE Leadership's training history. Someone gets introduced to the business, gets involved, and begins contacting people. But he or she never takes the time to make a written list. Invariably, this LIFE Member forgets a few but doesn't even realize it until he or she sees one of those people at an event somewhere—involved with *somebody else*! "Why didn't you call me about this?" the person usually asks, to which there can be no good answer. "I forgot about you" isn't something anyone wants to hear! Don't make that mistake. Be a professional from the very start. Make a *written* list of names.

There is a strong tendency in the beginning for a LIFE Member to prejudge people. For one reason or another, people are left off the list or not considered as legitimate contacts. "They are rich already." "He would never do this." "He wouldn't listen to me." "She's too busy." "That person isn't interested in personal growth." Again, let us give a warning: *Do not prejudge people.* Stories abound of big leaders who were on somebody's list but were never contacted for reasons just like these. Then, they eventually joined with somebody else and built a large business. Those are the kind of mistakes nobody wants to think about. The best way to avoid such an enormous loss of potential is to refrain from prejudging anybody and to give people the chance to determine for themselves if they are interested in the lifestyle available through LIFE Leadership and its informational products.

Once the names list is constructed, it is a good idea to do two things with it. First, rearrange the names according to what might be called "affinity groups." These are groups of people that know each other already. Second, try to identify the most ambitious people on the list. There doesn't seem to be any ideal characteristic of one who will be most successful at community building, but there are four attributes common to the most successful business builders:

1. Ambitious
2. Looking
3. Teachable
4. Honest

Whenever a person meeting this description is exposed to LIFE Leadership, he or she generally gets involved. But these characteristics are not easy to identify. At this point, simply make a guess. Some people *are* more ambitious than others. Some *are* looking for more in life. Some *are* more teachable than others. And finally, some *are* honest, and some are not (unfortunately). Be careful not to turn this into prejudging; it is just a best guess as to where you should *begin*.

Throughout the years of building your business, the names list is to be a living, breathing document. It should be updated constantly with new names and contacts. It is a good idea to revisit this brainstorming exercise at least once a month to make sure you haven't forgotten anybody.

Contacting

A list of names is good, but by itself, it accomplishes nothing. We have seen people craft a beautiful list of names but then do nothing with it. The purpose of generating a list of names in the first place is to get those names *off* that list, and this is accomplished through *contacting*.

Contacting is the initial connection to the business for the people on your list. It is very important, so much so that many feel as much as 50 percent of enrolling a new LIFE Member depends on the contact. This is because it is the new person's first impression of the concept.

The purpose of the contacting step is not to explain a bunch of stuff. It is *not* to convince people to buy LIFE Leadership materials or join your business. It is not to tell them all about it. **The purpose of the contacting step is simply to *book an appointment.*** The reason for this is that your business cannot be properly portrayed by words. It must be demonstrated. LIFE Leadership must be given the explanation it deserves. LIFE Leadership is a fantastic economic opportunity. It is right in the middle of four major industries. For these reasons and more, it is important to offer each prospect your business in a way that is the most relevant and as professional as possible. This is one of those points in the journey that LIFE Members just naturally mess up. There is a tendency to try to explain the concept or talk about it when all that is necessary is an appointment in the calendar. For that reason, allow us to reiterate: **The purpose of contacting is to book an appointment.**

How is this done? Again, too often LIFE Members quickly go off track here. They think they know best how to contact their acquaintances and friends. But experience has shown that people, left to their own "knowledge," will do exactly the wrong thing just about every time. Remember, this industry doesn't necessarily build the way you might think it does. So make the decision early to follow proven strategies. It will save you a lot of time and anguish.

There are two types of events to invite a prospect to attend. The first is a one-on-one plan. The second is a house plan. One-on-ones involve one couple or individual talking to another couple or individual. This is usually accomplished using a sketchpad (available from the Shopping Center on lifeleadership.com or from your upline support team), which has simplified diagrams corresponding to each of the main points in the plan. House plans involve a gathering of prospects arranged so the plan can be presented to them as a group. This is usually done using a large flip chart (also available from your upline or on the website Shopping Center). The guidelines for contacting may vary a little depending on the particular type of event. Where this is the case, it will be explained accordingly. However, most of these principles of contacting are universal.

Let's talk about the principles first. Then we'll get to the specifics. Stay with us now. It's simple!

Principles of Contacting

Be Brief

Do not get involved in a lengthy discussion or get to the point where the prospect is asking a string of questions that you are scrambling to answer. Keep it short and simple. The best contact takes less than ninety seconds. As Tim Marks says, "Be bright, be brief, and be gone." Using a proven script will help you stay brief.

Create Curiosity

Say just enough to make the prospect(s) curious. Give them a good nugget or two that provides a little information about what you are doing, enough to get them curious, and then move on.

Qualify the Prospect

LIFE Leadership products are materials that can make a positive impact on anybody and everybody's lives; however, building communities is not for everyone. The best time to find this out is during the contact. For this reason, contacting someone who is not interested is not a waste of time; it is actually a time *saver*. Showing your business to someone who is not qualified is like trying to sell a bathing suit to a polar bear. A proper contact qualifies the prospect(s) to make sure they are at least a little ambitious and looking for something more in life. Remember that anyone who does not build a business with you can (and should) become a customer of the fantastic line of LIFE Leadership materials.

Posture

The contacting step should demonstrate your posture and belief in LIFE Leadership and its products. *Posture* is your mental stance or level of conviction about what you are doing; the higher your belief, the higher your posture. The more excited and enthusiastic you are, the higher your posture. Posture is communicated through your enthusiasm level, the excitement in your voice, the confidence and conviction with which you speak, and the assertiveness with which you conduct yourself. (Be careful. Just because you have posture doesn't mean you shouldn't be friendly and nice. Never become pushy or "salesy.") Somehow, prospects have built-in posture detectors. They get a "feeling" about you and what you are doing and representing. They know immediately if you believe in it. Therefore, it is important for you to have proper posture, which can be developed by immersing yourself in the LIFE Training materials. Listen to audios on a regular basis, and subscribe to the Maximum Theory: Don't try to discover the *minimum* amount of listening that will bring success; go for the *maximum*! That is one of the fastest ways to develop belief and conviction in your business.

Posture is further developed as you gain experience rotating each of the five steps in the pattern. The more you listen, attend, read, learn, and do, the higher your posture and the better your results.

It is possible to have too much posture, just as it is possible to have too little posture. Too much posture makes you appear pushy. Too little posture makes you appear weak and unconvinced about your business. As we sometimes say, the correct level of posture is somewhere between "wimp" on one side and "jerk" on the other.

Activity, Part One

One important thing to do before making contacts is to put yourself in the right frame of mind. This involves reminding yourself who you are and why you are building your business in the first place. Think about your dreams and all the things you want to accomplish through LIFE Leadership. Then think about your dreads and all the things you'd like to improve, change, or get away from in your current situation. As a general rule, we should never get too far away from our reason *why*, and this is doubly true when we are making contacts. Your dreams will fuel you to take the action steps necessary to build your business.

Next (and perhaps first), think about what a great opportunity you are offering to the people you are about to contact (whether you are calling to sell some of the products or subscriptions or to interest them in the business itself—because both have the potential to be *life-changing*). If it's good enough for you, it will be good enough for them, too. If it has changed your life and given you new hopes and dreams, wouldn't they awaken to the same great things if given the chance and the same information you've received? Of course! And that's the chance you are about to offer them as you make the call. Picture having a big business and accomplishing your dreams. Would you hesitate to call someone about such a great business if it had already worked for you? Or consider how the information provided by the products has helped improve your life. Wouldn't they love to benefit from the same?

Another helpful mental preparation is the following: Develop the frame of mind that you are a multimillion-dollar business owner, and you are making contact with potential new partners in the venture. It is as if you are calling to arrange an interview. If they are not interested, no big deal. If they are interested, great!

Either way, you are going to fill the position(s). As you build your business, remember, you don't need any one particular person. No one is "your guy," your key to success. You can't lead anyone you *need*. That's posture, and these are just some of the ways to put yourself into the right posture when contacting.

Obtain a Written Appointment

One of the most effective tools in the LIFE Training system is the LIFE Leadership Calendar (stock number TL 113E for the full-size calendar and TL 220D for the pocket-size calendar). Your contact should end with an appointment written into both your calendar *and* the calendar of the prospect(s). A loose appointment is no appointment. The most successful leaders use this written calendar to track their business growth indicators (goals, plans shown, and results) all on one page. This is also the best way to PDCA (Plan, Do, Check, and Adjust) with your mentor; you both can look back at the previous month's activity and see if your efforts match your goals/commitments.

Make the Appointment Soon

The appointment should not be too far into the future. The more time between your initial contact and the appointment, the more likely a cancellation or "no show" will occur.

Make No Confirmation Calls

The appointment should require no confirmation call. A booked appointment is a booked appointment. You will be there when you said you will be there. Do not allow yourself to get trapped in a situation where the prospect says to you, "Call me to confirm" or "Give me a call, and we'll figure out the time." The appointment should be booked for a specific time and place, and no further phone calls or conversations are necessary. We have found that a call to confirm is an invitation for a cancellation.

Answer Questions with Questions

It is best to answer a question with a question. This is easier if you have a few response questions memorized ahead of time. We'll make some suggestions for this in a moment.

Make Appointments at the Prospect's Home

This principle is specific to one-on-ones. Always try to make the appointment at the *prospect's house*. People feel the most comfortable and hospitable in their own homes. Although their home environment may possibly be a little distracting to you (small children, dogs, mother-in-laws, etc.), it isn't distracting to *them* (except for perhaps the mother-in-law). Your best chance of getting a prospect to listen is if you have the appointment at his or her house. The worst chance for a successful meeting is if you book the appointment at his or her place of employment. First of all, it isn't too professional because he or she is there to do a job, and you are potentially interfering with that responsibility. But of even bigger concern is the way people behave when they are sitting behind their own desk, playing the big shot, dictating terms to anybody who sits on the other side of it. Only slightly better are appointments at restaurants. This is because there are distractions galore, and restaurants are very easy locations for prospects *not* to go! More than once have we sat in a restaurant, sipping our water, telling the waitress to wait just a few more minutes for that person we're sure is going to arrive at any minute.

Have the Prospect's Spouse Present for the Plan

When a prospect is married, always try to have his or her spouse present at the appointment. This is critical because it doubles the odds of having somebody get excited. Not every couple comes into your business or starts buying your products with the same level of enthusiasm on the part of both spouses. As with all decisions (getting married, having children, learning to salsa dance, etc.), usually one spouse is more interested in the idea than the other. It is only natural. Showing the plan to *both* partners at the same time increases the chance of getting at least one of them excited. Additionally, it ensures that whoever "wears the pants" in the family will see the big picture, too. Time and again, we have seen people get one spouse fired up, but when that spouse went home and tried to relate his or her excitement, he or she got shot down before even getting started. "The boss" squelched the idea in its infancy. This is because *prospects* don't know how to properly present the plan yet. *You* are the professional (or are hopefully becoming one)! You should be the one to explain it to all potential partners.

Contact in Batches

Contacting is most effective when done in batches. It may be helpful to think of the word *blitz* when contacting. Generally, the more contacts you complete in a short amount of time, the better you will do. This is because you will be in practice and not rusty. Sometimes we hear people say, "I've set a goal to make one contact a day." While that is a worthy goal, the likelihood is that most of those contacts will be done when the business owner is not warmed up. Making several contacts in a row can develop a momentum that actually increases results. For that reason, clump your contacts together. Make several at the same time. Fill your calendar with appointments all in one shot.

Activity, Part One

Over-Invite People for Group Meetings

This principle is specific to group meetings. Always invite more people than you want to attend. This is because not all the people who commit to attending will be able to make it. Some will have legitimate reasons for missing the appointment. Others will simply be too nice to say no on the phone even though they are really not interested. Invite at least twice the number of people you would actually like to have in attendance. (We will talk in more detail about conducting house plans in the next chapter.)

These are the main principles involved in contacting. Understanding them—and sticking to them—will play a big part in your success.

Specifics of Contacting

The specifics of contacting build on the principles. There are three specific ways people can be contacted about your business. The first is what we might call a physical contact. This is one in which you telephone prospects or speak to them in person (although we usually recommend calling). The second method of contacting is done by exposing prospects to the LIFE Leadership products. The final method involves exposing them to LIFE Training materials or meetings.

Circles of Influence

Prior to digging into the details of contacting, it may help to illustrate your circle of influence and what it means to build a community. Influence is based, in part, on trust and relationships with others. So the easiest and simplest way to start contacting is with people who already know and respect you, namely, family and close friends. We like to explain it with two questions: "Who's your daddy?" and "Who's your Ethel?" Everybody has a family member who would be willing to listen to his or her business plan. And just like in the old TV show *I Love Lucy*, in which Lucy always had a friend (Ethel) involved with her in any caper that she got herself into, most people have an Ethel or two in their lives! So to get started contacting, answer the questions "Who's your daddy?" and "Who's your Ethel?"

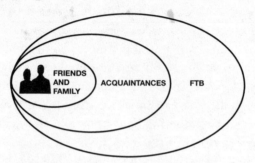

The next group is people with whom you associate through work, church, or other activities. You know them by name, and they know you. But you are not necessarily close friends; you are acquaintances instead. The last group is the biggest list you have: friends to be (FTB). This is the biggest list (actually infinite) because you meet people every day. Over time, these people may move into the acquaintances circle, while some may even move into the close friends circle. The old saying "A stranger is just a friend I haven't met yet" applies here. Keep moving people from the FTB and acquaintances circles closer to the friends circle, and you will discover *the* greatest treasures of this journey: abundant and rich relationships!

Contacting Family and Close Friends

To begin contacting, keep in mind that a complicated question elicits a complicated answer, but a simple question elicits a simple answer. So when contacting (especially family and close friends), keep it simple! If you don't, you could get trapped into explaining everything to your sister or best friend (and you *don't* want to do that). Here are a few examples:

> "Did I catch you at a bad time? Are you going to be around in twenty minutes? I've got something I ***need*** to drop off to you."

(This particular approach is utilized when using LIFE Leadership products to make a contact. More on this in a moment.)

Or

"I've come across something exciting, and I want to share it with you!"

(This particular approach is utilized when directly booking an appointment over the phone.)

Or for scheduling a house plan at your house:

"I've come across something exciting, and I want you to come over here _____ night at _____ so I can share it with you!"

Remember, the key to contacting family and close friends is to be excited, be natural, and keep it brief.

Contacting with a Script

One effective way to make the initial contact is either over the phone or face to face in a quick, to-the-point conversation. A contacting script works best with the larger circles of influence: *acquaintances and FTB*. A contacting script is a prewritten approach that has been proven to work. We recommend following one as closely as possible. (You may download proven scripts from the LIFE Training portion of the website, or check with your upline support team). Again, we often hear people say things like, "But that will sound corny to people who know me" or "I could never say that." So they proceed to contact people using their own approach and experience poor results. Eventually, they try a proven script and are amazed at the difference. Scripts work. The words have been chosen carefully, and the entire structure has been developed through thousands of real-life contacts. *As an example,* the following is a script that has been proven to be very successful:

> "Hello, (*prospect's name*). This is (*your name*). Have I caught you at a bad time?" (*If yes, ask when would be a good time to call again. Some things are too obvious, aren't they?*)

> "Great, well, the reason I'm calling is I fell in with a couple guys who are pioneering an information marketing business (or leadership development business or personal development business) online. They're expanding right now, and I thought of you. I can't promise anything, but I'd like to get together and discuss the details. How's Wednesday night at eight?"

> 1. (*The prospect may ask*): "What is it?" (*or something similar*).

> (*To which you answer with a question*): "Have you heard of Robert Kiyosaki's Cashflow Quadrant? It'll make more sense when we get together. How's Wednesday at eight?"

> 2. (*Next the prospect may ask*): "Is this one of those pyramid deals?" (*or something similar*).

> (*To which you answer with a question*): "Have you heard of Michael Dell's 3 Cs? It'll make more sense when we get together. How's Wednesday at eight?"

> 3. (*Next the prospect may ask*): "Is this network marketing?" (*or something similar*).

> (*To which you answer with a question*): "Have you heard of (*insert your upline's name here*)? It will make a lot more sense when we get together. How's Wednesday at eight?"

Activity, Part One

(If he or she persists with questions and won't book the appointment, say):

"Well, I tell you what, *(prospect's name)*. It doesn't sound like you're open to looking at anything right now. Why don't we just forget it. If you ever change your mind, give me a call. Right now, I've got to go."

(Or if you'd like to try one last approach, say the following):

"Well, I tell you what, *(prospect's name)*. It sounds like I have somehow given you the wrong impression. I apologize. Are you going to be home for about twenty minutes? How about if I just drop something off to you?"

(If choosing this approach, then you are simply bailing on the telephone contact and switching to a product contact—to be explained momentarily).

(Now, going back to the original statement when you first got the person on the phone, if the prospect answers): "Yes" *(that he or she has heard of whatever you stated first, say)*:

"Great! So are you already making money with it?"

(To which he or she will most likely respond with more questions or with a simple): "No."

(At this point, you simply say): "Well, I'll show you what we're doing with it when we get together. How's Wednesday at eight?"

This script, or something very close to it, will work. (Again, see the LIFE Training portion of the website for up-to-date scripts). Be very careful before making any changes to it. Get the input of your experienced, higher level upline before making alterations. Sometimes, one or two simple word changes are all that is necessary to reduce its effectiveness. So be careful. Rehearse this script over and over by reading it aloud to yourself. Practice so that it doesn't sound scripted. Eventually, you will get to where you can contact without even thinking about it. But especially in the beginning, be sure and use the script. Have these words in front of you. Open this book to these pages, or use a downloaded script and have it close at hand as you make your calls. The closer you stay to the words of a proven script, the higher your success rate at booking appointments.

As we indicated, the above script is designed primarily for inviting prospects to see the plan in a one-on-one setting. With minor modifications, this same script works well when inviting prospects to house plans. After asking "How's _____ night at _____ o'clock?" inform them of the location of the house plan. "Great. It's at my house. Do you remember how to get here?" (if the question is applicable). If the house plan is at someone else's home instead of yours, it is a good idea to offer to pick up your prospects. Very few people feel comfortable just walking into a stranger's home. Besides, there is a much higher possibility of them actually showing up if you pick them up! These simple details can easily be arranged within the body of the above script. The key is to accomplish the major objectives of the contact and get them to see the plan.

Contacting with Phone Call Sessions/Business Launches

Another specific way to contact prospective new customers and business owners is through an event called a phone call or contacting session, or what is more commonly referred to as a business launch. At these gatherings, groups of LIFE Members get together and make a bunch of contacts all at once and record their results on a board for all to see. Friendly competitions can be arranged during which participants break up into teams to see who can book the most appointments. Prizes can be awarded for individual and team achievement.

The reason business launches are so popular and work so effectively is because people are encouraged by the performance of others. When we see our partners making calls and getting results, it inspires us to do the same. There is power in a group of like-minded individuals all running for their goals and dreams together. Contacting is well enabled by this group inertia. Also, competition is fun and can spur us onward. Where we may hesitate to sit by ourselves and break through mental barriers, the heat of a competition, even if it's to determine who buys the pizza or ice cream, can push us out of our shell and compel us to act. Usually, once people have participated in a phone call session and proven to themselves that they can make contacts successfully, it is easier for them to continue making calls on their own later. This is because the business launch helped build their belief. The people at a business launch see their business working right before their very eyes. They see others having success. They see firsthand that the contacting scripts work. These experiences give new business owners confidence that they can achieve success also.

Business launches can be a good way to spark a particular group of LIFE Members into action. If leaders review their group and decide that not enough plans are being shown in a given location, they can host a business launch to help get things moving. This provides an excellent format for training, answering questions, associating, and building confidence. Most important though, business launches work. Entire organizations wouldn't exist today if someone hadn't gathered together a group of business owners and initiated a business launch to get things moving. If such an event becomes available to you, be sure to take advantage of it.

Contacting with Products

One of the immense benefits of LIFE Leadership is the marketability of its products. With LIFE Leadership, you have premier, life-changing informational materials at your disposal that can themselves be used as contacting tools. What better way to introduce someone to your business than through your product(s)?

Here's how it goes.

When you call your prospect(s), ask them if they are going to be home for the next twenty minutes or so, saying, "I've got something I need to drop off to you." Then pull up in their driveway and leave the engine running and the car door open, clearly indicating that you aren't necessarily planning on staying. Walk up to the house and hand them one of the LIFE Leadership materials, whether an individual CD or a pack (check with your upline for what is working best at the moment). The beauty of the LIFE Leadership materials, categorized as they are into each of the 8 Fs, is that you can select a CD or pack from the category in which you know the person may be looking for something more. Are they struggling financially? Then hand them something from the Finances category. Are they active in their community and interested in national affairs? Hand them something from the Freedom category. This can be applied to any of the 8 Fs. However, you can also hand them a pack covering all 8 Fs (such as the *8 F Introductory Pack*), allowing them to select their own category of primary interest. Or you can use one of the introductory CDs (designed specifically for this purpose) that introduce the *Mental Fitness Challenge*, one of LIFE Leadership's flagship products. Again, check with your upline to see what is being used most effectively at the moment. Then proceed to book the appointment at which you will return to show them the plan.

The goal of sharing some of the LIFE Leadership materials in this way is to break the ice in order to book an appointment at which you will show the plan. However, sometimes when sharing the product and getting a question or two, you can immediately show the plan (see chapter six) right then and there! Why wait? However, if time or circumstances will not permit, your alternative is to book a solid appointment to show the plan later. In either case, **it is vital to schedule solid appointments** and to avoid saying things like, "I will call you later about it."

By using products to initiate contacts, you are also demonstrating a method of building your business that the new people joining your team will remember and easily be able to duplicate. That is why you are encouraged to always have an ample supply of LIFE Leadership materials on hand. In effect, these products become your advertising. As the saying goes, "If you're out of product, you're out of business." Make sure you always have some LIFE Leadership products to hand out to others.

Contacting with products is very well received in the marketplace. For some reason, prospects seem to respond very well to an initial contact made with the LIFE Leadership materials. It's as if they instinctively want to get excited about the business by first being introduced to the products. There are stories galore of people not being interested in the business, per se, until they became enthusiastic about the materials. So learn this approach well. Share the products with people and let it break the ice! It's as simple as saying, "Hi. Here!"

Contacting with the LIFE Training Marketing System

Perhaps the least common, but still effective, method of contacting people is by exposing them to the exciting training materials from the LIFE Training Marketing System. This might occur if someone has the opportunity to listen to an audio or browse through one of the pamphlets. This is very similar to what happens when you contact someone directly with the LIFE Leadership materials. But generally, this contact happens more by accident. "What's this?" they usually ask, to which the LIFE Member then responds according to the principles we discussed and books an appointment at which to show the plan or simply shows it right then and there. There are many stories about people who got into the business because the driver of the car in which they were car pooling was listening to audios from LIFE Training, or perhaps they saw one of the LIFE Leadership videos playing in someone's living room. Remember, truth is sweet to the ears. If people are looking for a better life and get exposed to the truths in our system, they will usually be interested in learning more.

Summary

Making a list of names and then contacting those people to book appointments are very important steps to building LIFE Leadership. Without becoming adept at both of these steps, it will be very difficult to build a strong and profitable business. Take the time to develop proficiency. Become a professional. Update your names list frequently, and make contacts to book appointments on a regular basis. At first, your upline support team will help you. Eventually though, you need to take over the helm of the ship. After all, it's your business. The sooner you master these first two steps, the sooner you'll be ready to move on to the next three, which begin with the most important of all: showing the plan.

*Success lies in forming the habit of doing things
that failures don't like to do.*
—Albert Gray

Only do what only you can do.
—Unknown

Never judge a person's horsepower by his exhaust.
—Unknown

*Opportunity is missed by most people because it is dressed in
overalls and looks like work.*
—Unknown (sometimes attributed to Thomas Edison)

Don't wait for your ship to come in; swim out to it.
—Unknown

Name: COOL GUY CARL

Quote: "My man, I have nine different ways to become a millionaire already. Besides, I'm way too cool to do something like that!"

CHAPTER 6

ACTIVITY, PART TWO
SHOWING THE PLAN

After making a list and contacting, the remaining steps in the Five-Step Pattern are:

3. Showing the Plan
4. Following Through
5. Getting Them Started (Rotating the Pattern)

The purpose of the contact is to book an appointment, and the purpose of the appointment is to show the plan. This is where the rubber meets the road. Showing the plan is the most constructive part of building LIFE Leadership. As far as we can tell, people who don't have the plan shown to them don't get into the business! Therefore, to build your business bigger, you will need to show the plan! This chapter will deal exclusively with that step of the process.

House Plans and One-on-Ones

There are generally two types of plans to be shown, as we covered only slightly in the last chapter. A *one-on-one* is when an individual or couple presents the plan to another individual or couple. The second type of plan is called a *house plan*. This is where several people are invited to someone's home to see the plan in a group setting.

House Plans

House plans (also called group meetings) are by far the most efficient way to share your business with prospective LIFE Members.

71

This is because house plans require showing just one plan, but several people get to see it at once. For this reason, house plans are the plan of choice. To build a team fast, house plans must be a regular occurrence in the team builder's calendar. To build your business without an avid use of house plans is to paddle a canoe with a serving spoon (or perhaps even a teaspoon).

There are many ways to make a house plan effective. First of all, the newest, most excited, *deepest* (furthest down the leg in an organization) LIFE Member should be the one to host such an event. However, this doesn't have to be the case. The leading business builder should make sure that this host couple or individual is properly assisted in building a names list and in *contacting more than enough prospects* from that list. Next, the leader can invite other LIFE Members that are in the upline of the host individual or couple to "plug into" that house plan. Possibly, this invitation can be conditional; for example, only those LIFE Members who can also bring new prospects to the house plan are invited. Finally, the leader can then plug in some individuals from his or her other organizations. This will demonstrate how a proper house plan should run and give people a chance to build their belief, gain some time around an excited group of people, and build a better relationship with the leader (in this example, the one showing the plan). This may be a bit too involved to delve into further here, but remember, once you get to that point, make house plans the cornerstone of your business and pack everything into them that you can to make them as effective as possible in building your business.

One-on-Ones

One-on-ones are the "filler" in a business builder's calendar. They are used when it is temporarily not possible to set up an effective house plan in an area or when it simply works out to show a certain individual the plan. One-on-ones should not be avoided, however, but rather they should be used aggressively to develop a cluster of people, both LIFE Members and interested parties, that can then participate in an upcoming house plan that brings it all together. In other words: one-on-ones support an upcoming house plan.

House plans and one-on-one plans are slightly different in their setup and how they are conducted. Each will be addressed individually in the discussions to follow. As in the previous chapter, we will talk about *principles* of showing the plan first, with *specifics* to follow.

Principles of Showing the Plan

There are several resources that can assist you in learning the principles of showing the plan. Of course, the aforementioned "How to Get Started" materials are a great place to begin. A further perspective on showing the plan can be gained by listening to audio recordings dealing specifically with that subject. What you will discover is that there are five main purposes of showing the plan:

1. Make a friend.
2. Find a need.
3. Transfer the feeling.
4. Involve them in the system and the product.
5. Book a follow-through.

Make a Friend

This entire industry is built on relationships. That is why there is so much emphasis in the LIFE Training Marketing System on people skills and personal growth. If one isn't relatable and like-able, there will be no basis for starting a new relationship and, therefore, very little chance of growing a business.

The first objective in showing the plan is to become friends with the prospect(s). This is not a technique or trick; it must be done sincerely and on a real, personal level. It begins by listening—one of life's most important, but also most rare, skills. It should be a major objective of the business owner to ask questions and get to know the prospect(s). Looking around their home as you prepare to show them the plan also reveals immense clues about who they are and what activities they pursue. Are there trophies on the mantle? Is there a snowmobile trailer in the driveway? Is their home decorated with photos of children and/ or grandchildren? The point is to be attentive. Pay attention to others. Ask and listen and learn. The objective is to get to know them. Make a friend with each prospect.

There is an old sying in the sales world: "You cannot sell John Brown what John Brown buys until you can see the world through John Brown's eyes." That's a little of what is happening here. The plan should be tailored to the individual(s) to whom you are showing it. To do that properly, you must understand a little about the person(s) on the receiving end.

Further, for friendship to begin, the prospect(s) must also begin to like you. Relatability is the quality that endears you to others and helps you make a good first impression. The prospect(s) should feel at ease with you and should feel that you are "real." Remember, nobody will enter into a business arrangement with someone they don't know, like, and trust. Relatability is the ability to arrive at these three qualities in the eyes of the prospect(s).

Unless the first objective of "making a friend" is reached, it is not only futile but *impossible* to move on to the second objective. So the first part of showing the plan is to make friends with the prospect(s). This must happen. If it *doesn't*, the rest of the steps either won't take place or will likely be in vain.

Find a Need

The second objective of showing the plan is to find out what the prospect(s) want. This is usually called a dream. What we have found, as discussed earlier, is that people often have extensive lists of wants or fantasies that they say they want but for which they are not willing to work. What must be done at this step is to identify the true desires of their heart. What do they *really* want? A dream is something that a person needs to have fulfilled in his or her life. That's why we say at this step to find a *need*. What condition, helped by money and time and more personal freedom, do the prospect(s) long for in their life that won't come true without LIFE Leadership? What would they do if they won the lottery? What is the true motivation of their heart?

This may sound harder to find than it actually is. Most people are dreamers. Most people have deep yearnings for more time with their family, alleviation of debt, more security in their financial future, more friends and social opportunities, more relationships—all the types of results that your business can provide! This is why it is so important in the above step to make a connection with the prospect(s) because as you get to know them, you will come to understand what motivates them. It will be easier to identify what rewards would make your business worth it for them.

Often we'll hear people say, "I just couldn't get a dream out of them" or "They really didn't seem to want anything." These might very well be true. But more often, the reason prospect(s) are closed-lipped about their dreams is because the business owner hasn't taken the time to initiate a relationship. If the prospect(s) don't know, like, and trust you, they will not open up to you about their dreams and desires. Period. Also, as Amy Marks says, "Discovering someone's dream is hard if we don't have one of our own!" Make sure *your* dreams are alive and vibrant, and that will help others open up about *their* dreams.

Remember, people will not join your business if someone doesn't help them identify what's in it for them. Help them find their reason *why*, and you will help them find their way to it.

What's in it for them?

What's in it for them?

What's in it for them?

Never get more than a couple of seconds away from that question!

Transfer the Feeling

After connecting with the prospect(s), initiating a relationship, and identifying what they are looking for more of in life, next it is important to transfer a feeling of excitement and belief. Even if the prospect(s) like you, and even if they have legitimate goals and dreams they are willing to work to achieve, if you bore them to tears, they probably won't want to become your business partner.

We cannot overemphasize the importance of enthusiasm. When contacting, showing the plan, in fact, during every step of the Five-Step Pattern, it is vitally important to be enthusiastic and excited. If your business is the best opportunity for your prospect(s), if it is going to wipe out debt and allow early retirement and provide freedom and financial stability and all the dreams and goals we talk about, then it makes sense that you should be commensurably excited about it. Your enthusiasm has to match your message. Granted, if you were showing up to explain that you can help them make $3.50 a month, enthusiasm would be a little out of place. But, obviously, you are offering so much more than that. Your excitement should communicate that all by itself.

Some personalities have no problem with this. They're the type to be cracking jokes at funerals. Other personalities think they are being exciting and showing enthusiasm, but everybody around them for three city blocks is falling asleep. It is important to know yourself and to which category you belong. Those whose enthusiasm is "over the top" *may* need to tone it down a bit and focus on being relatable. Those that are even *slightly* unenthusiastic must work to increase the level of excitement demonstrated. Don't underestimate the importance of this step. Attitudes and emotions are contagious. So if you're transferring a feeling, make sure it's positive! And if you're excited, be sure to notify your face!

Involve Them in the System and the Product

"The system" refers to the complete line of training materials (called "tools") and meetings provided by LIFE Training. Properly utilized, these are to be leveraged to increase your relatability and appeal.

It may be that you are already a very relatable person. You are doing a great job of connecting with your prospect(s), and you have identified a real need that your business can help them fulfill. But you still need to bring out the heavy artillery. You still need to leverage the LIFE Training materials and LIFE Leadership products to work on your behalf. There are many reasons for this.

First, excitement has a shelf life. Even if you did everything right when contacting and showing the plan, there is still the tendency of prospects to "cool off" after you have gone. Leaving behind and promoting the correct materials, such as the *First Night Pack*, and getting them to an Open Meeting will not only maintain the excitement level but will also *increase* it. Promote the first-night materials along with the rest of the LIFE Leadership materials to keep prospects involved and interested long after you have gone.

Second, you will only "click" with a small percentage of the people out there. We are all different. We all have our particular temperaments and interests. These variations make it likely that we'll bond quite naturally with some people but have to work much harder at it with others. This is where the LIFE Training system steps in. Different personalities, backgrounds, ethnicities, and religious beliefs are represented on the audios, in the books, and at the meetings. Even if a prospect doesn't exactly relate to *you*, he or she will certainly find something or someone within the materials and/or community that he or she *can* relate to. In this way, the system broadens your relatability and, therefore, your effectiveness.

Third, you can't possibly be everywhere at once, meeting the needs of an increasingly larger and larger organization and answering every question or need that arises. If you start people using the system as their source of answers right up front, you will create the proper habits on their part for finding the answers to their questions. They will seek the system as their teacher and not you. This frees up enormous amounts of your time and also establishes a duplicatable pattern that they can in turn follow. Duplication, after all, is the secret to the explosive growth potential of the concept of franchising.

"What do I do next?" they might ask.

"Exactly what I've done with you" is the answer.

"What tools do I leave them after I show them the plan?" they ask.

"The same ones I left for you."

"What do I do about leaving sample LIFE Leadership products?" they ask.

"The same as I did with you" is again the answer.

See how duplication works? Utilize the system and the products from the very beginning to bring people into your business, and you are already teaching them how to get started building their own business properly.

Book a Follow-Through

The fifth and final aspect to showing the plan is to book a "follow-through." A follow-through is the next meeting at which the business owner (you) will get back together with the prospect(s) and continue the process. We will explain more of how to conduct a follow-through later, but at this stage of showing the plan, it is critical that a solid time to get back together has been agreed upon by both parties and written down.

Many, many times, LIFE Members have done every step of the pattern correctly until this one. They make a great list. They do an excellent job of contacting and booking the appointment. They show an inspired, informed plan. But for some reason, at the end of the plan, they walk away from the prospect(s) without booking a solid time to get back together and continue the process. Don't make this fatal mistake. Don't leave the scene of the plan and say, "I'll call you." You might as well cross their names off your list right then and there; they will not get involved in your business. Most likely, you'll try to call them a couple of times and may or may not get in touch with them. Either way, you have lost posture, and now you are "chasing" them. When there is a loss of posture, the process is over. To avoid all of this, simply book an appointment before leaving the plan!

It even helps to let the prospect(s) know during the plan what the process will be. Tell them that today (the showing of the plan) is only the initial meeting. At the end of the plan, you will be booking a time to get back together with them to help them further assess their potential in the business. When prospective LIFE Members know what to expect, they are more likely to follow along.

Specifics of Showing the Plan

Understanding these general principles of showing the plan, it is now appropriate to paint in the details.

Dress

Showing up to present the business to someone is a chance to make a good first impression. So dress appropriately. Be a professional. For men, this means wearing at least "business casual" (no jeans), the most effective of which is a LIFE Leadership logo shirt and slacks. (I can't believe we just used the word *slacks*. What will we say next, *trousers*?) For women, it means nice slacks (there we go again!) and a conservative top. These are simple guidelines, but they are very effective.

People sometimes resist this, but again, the concept is to exercise professionalism and facilitate duplication. Deviation from this standard has incredible ramifications. First, the sloppier or crazier a man dresses, the less he relates to others. This has an enormous impact on sponsoring. For women, the more revealing or intimidating their appearance, the less they will be able to relate to other women, and the more they will distract men. Second, the more "off track" someone is in appearance, the more it will be duplicated by his or her organization. It doesn't take very many iterations before someone arrives to show the plan wearing a bathing suit. (You think we're kidding!) The point is this: Whether male or female, dress for *business*. This means that your attire doesn't draw attention to itself. Your clothing should be such that *it* isn't noticed; *you* and *what you have to present* are noticed instead. The resulting impression is one of friendly professionalism that doesn't intimidate.

Hygiene

We hate having to even discuss this, but next is the topic of proper hygiene. It should go without saying that one should show up to represent a business looking and acting the part of a business owner. This means proper appearance in personal grooming, as well as the considerations of dress just discussed.

What do we mean? A business owner should be showered, smelling good (but not overpowering), with teeth brushed, and wearing clean, pressed clothes. Hair should be neat and not the object of distraction or conversation. Fingernails should be clean and cut short. Visible piercings and corresponding jewelry should be minimized. Men should make sure they don't have wrinkled shirts or pants or armpit stains, and their nose and ear hair should be trimmed. (We're serious!) Facial hair has also historically been considered by many to be a possible distraction. Women should, well, women should ask their upline women leaders what they should do. (You didn't think we were stupid enough to say something here that would risk offending the entire female gender, did you? We may have been born at night, but it wasn't last night.) Conservative fit and style will avoid distracting anyone from the main message. Remember, all of this is intended to simply allow the business and your attitude as a professional LIFE Member to shine through rather than your appearance. We want people to remember the possibilities your business provides for their lives, not odd features of personal appearance, dress, or grooming (or lack thereof).

This is all just common sense. And we are certain that you, the reader, already knew all of this stuff, so you certainly won't get insulted by our mentioning a few of these recommendations. After all, they will help the people on *your team* who *might* need to hear them. For the people to which some of these things might apply: We, the humble authors, can't possibly know who is reading these words right now. We aren't even around! So there is no reason to take offense. We don't even know it's you this instruction was meant for! (Wow! This is tough!) Let's move on.

First Impressions

Another very important thing to consider when arriving to show the plan, whether to an individual, couple, or house full of people, is to be conscious of your first impression. The old saying "You'll never get a second chance to make a good first impression" rings true.

Here are some specifics that we hope will be helpful.

First, lead with a smile. You'd be surprised what barriers can be broken down with a simple, sincere, confident smile. A smile lets other people know you are at ease, confident, and open to them. Make it a practice to smile before you ever say a word to anyone. Become accustomed to smiling the moment someone looks at you. These things will take practice, but you will notice enormous results by the simple art of smiling. Dale Carnegie, perhaps the most famous teacher ever of people skills, ranks smiling at the top of the list of importance in human relations. So lead with a smile in everything you do.

Second, make eye contact. It has been said that the eyes are the window to the soul. Looking people in the eyes lets them know you are fully engaged and focused on them and what they are saying. It also gives you a great chance to "read" them and pick up on any non-verbal clues that will help you connect with them.

Third, learn to make a good hand shake. Don't be a "dead fish" (limp and light) or a "vise" (bone crusher) but rather somewhere in between. Also, avoid pumping someone's hand up and down repeatedly. We are making friends, not pumping water from a well! Stay away from pulling others into you when shaking hands and letting go too early or too late. Remember, you are in business. Hand shaking will be common in almost every interaction here, and your handshake is a chance to show that you are a professional.

Fourth, beware of overtalking, interrupting, close talking, and any other irritating talking maladies of which you may be guilty. We have all had to work on these from time to time, and it is a good idea to keep ourselves aware of the best conduct for endearing others to ourselves. Our favorite Tim Marks quote that should be helpful in this category is, "Just because it happened to you, doesn't make it interesting!" (Ouch!)

This whole category of first impressions will be addressed repeatedly in the books and audios on people skills available from LIFE Leadership. It is safe to say that no matter how adept in dealing with people that we become and no matter how high we progress in the business financially, it is never time to relax on the basic principles of getting along with people and being courteous. We should all read and learn about the great principles and specifics of people skills on a regular basis.

Environment

For One-on-One Plans

We discussed in the chapter on contacting how important it is to try to schedule the appointment for a one-on-one at the prospect's home. Assuming this has been accomplished, there are a couple of important related details.

Show up on time. Tardiness is a sign of a lack of discipline, disrespect for the other person(s), or both. Be prompt. Please note, though, that this does not mean be early. You don't want to appear eager or as if you have nothing better to do than to visit them that evening. Besides, there are some who believe being early is just as rude as being late.

Enter their home with respect, and never forget that you are a guest. Greet them at the door with a handshake, and as you enter, notice if they would like you to remove your shoes, etc. Introduce your spouse, and get an introduction to their spouse. Remember, small courtesies go a long way toward making friends. Pet their dog. Say hello to any children that come around. Be interested in their family. When you pull up to their home, don't take the parking spot(s) that are obviously theirs or box them in.

Next, direct the meeting to take place at their kitchen table. Don't let them set you down on couches or quarantine you to some formal living room. Simply say, "You know what? Would you mind if we used your kitchen table?" Most people are very cordial and hospitable. They will likely offer you a snack or something. The general rule is to always accept. It allows them to serve you a little and makes them feel a bit more at ease.

Don't get distracted or annoyed at interruptions. The patience you show with their household is a sign of respect that they will appreciate.

For House Plans

New LIFE Members usually give their business the fastest start by hosting a house plan. This is a situation in which their upline leader comes to their home to show the plan to friends and family on their behalf.

Let's consider the arrangement of the room. The board and easel with the flip chart should be placed at the opposite end of the room from where people enter. This minimizes distractions. For the same reason, children should be out of the room and with babysitters, preferably at a different location. Pets should be tucked away in another room where they can't get into the crowd of people and cause distraction. The best plan presenter in the world cannot compete with a cute child or friendly pet (not to mention the distraction inherent in a not-so-cute child or unfriendly pet).

The homeowner or host of the house plan should be very careful regarding his or her conduct. It has the biggest impact on the attitude and interest level of prospective new LIFE Members. For instance, as the time to begin the presentation draws near, the host should never say things like, "I expected more people than this" or "I can't believe John isn't here" or "They said they would be here." These seemingly harmless little statements kill the interest of the prospects that *are* on hand to see your business. It makes them wonder what's wrong with *them*. For the same reason, the host should not set out too many chairs in advance. It is much better to bring chairs out as people arrive than to have a bunch of empty chairs when the meeting begins. In general, the host should be excited, friendly, and professional.

The LIFE Member showing the plan should arrive at exactly ten minutes after the starting time. This is because the main speaker doesn't want to be forced into small talk with prospects before sharing the plan because it diminishes posture. (The homeowner should be informed of this in advance, so he or she isn't concerned when the presenter is ten minutes "late.") When the presenter arrives, he or she should be greeted by the meeting's host (usually the homeowner), who should help carry the board, easel, and flip chart inside to set them up. The host should then introduce the presenter to the group. A proper introduction should focus on the plan presenter, *not* the business itself. The host should describe the accomplishments of the presenter in verbiage that the audience can understand and relate to, the purpose being to create a desire on the part of each of the prospects to listen to what the presenter has to share. The feeling of the crowd ought to be, "Wow! I can't wait to hear what this person has to say!"

Perhaps an example is in order. A proper introduction of a house plan speaker should go something like this: "Hello, everybody. I have the honor tonight to introduce our speaker. This gentleman has his master's degree in engineering, was a senior engineer in the auto industry, and then got involved in what he's going to show you tonight. He has an enormous business and has been recognized for hitting some of the highest levels in this industry. His wife was able to leave her job because of the income they now make through this industry. And we've got him here tonight! We are very glad he could make it here to our house tonight. Please help me welcome Mr. _____." Often the person being introduced doesn't have the long list of credentials like the person in this example. In that case, it is still important to edify the person, *not* the business. This is done by making truthful statements like "He is wise beyond his years" or "His entrepreneurial spirit was evident when he started his own lawn-mowing business at the age of sixteen. He is an incredible student of leadership books and is learning directly from some of this industry's most successful business owners. I'm excited to be learning from him tonight." Obviously, the introduction should be changed to fit the exact qualifications of the speaker, but these examples should serve as a guide. Remember to introduce the *speaker* and not the *business*.

Content

Now it's time to consider the content of the plan itself. *You* or imperative sentences in this chapter refer to the person showing the plan. Remember, though, that the content of the plan isn't nearly as important as your attitude, enthusiasm, and posture during it. Some people get hung up on teaching all the details or hitting every segment of the plan just right. *It is not the plan that counts; it's the connection with the prospect(s).* The most successful plan presenters are not the ones who get every detail right and hit all the points. The most successful are the ones who connect the best with people and demonstrate relevancy to the prospects' dreams.

Also, don't get too hung up on learning each of the following particulars. The flip chart (for house plans) and sketchpad (for one-on-ones) are available to guide you through all of the following content. These are available on the Shopping Center at lifeleadership.com or from your upline. The flip charts provide a crutch, making it easy to get through the material without having to prepare a presentation or memorize information. Also, and this is very important, the flip chart and sketchpad are so easy and so duplicatable that prospects will immediately realize that they can do the very same thing you are doing.

For one-on-ones in particular: Once getting seated at the kitchen table as described above, initiate the process with some questions to get to know the prospect(s). Ask them about their family. Ask them about anything you spotted in their home that suggests their interests and hobbies. Ask them about their profession. A good acronym that may be of help here is "FORM," which stands for Family, Occupation, Recreation, and Message. The first three are great areas to cover before arriving at the "message" you want to share. If the prospect(s) are good friends or family members, obviously this part of the process is unnecessary. (But it would be funny to try!) Also, this step is not really possible at house plans.

The purpose of this conversation at the beginning of a one-on-one is for you to find out about the prospect(s). What are their strengths? What have they already accomplished in life? What is their worldview? Specifically, what things about them can you find out that allow you to be able to believe in their success? This is not some cryptic technique but a sincere attempt to get to know the prospect(s). You must find out some things about them so you can show them why LIFE Leadership will work for them. This is also where you might gain some insight into their dreams and aspirations.

This up-front conversation portion is important, but it doesn't have to take too long. It lasts just long enough for you to get to know them a little bit and to show an interest in them. Still, it might take a few minutes, so your time might be a little limited. It will not and should not be possible to show the whole plan during a one-on-one, talking in detail about each and every slide in the flip chart. Instead, you are just trying to hit the highlights. The concept is to "show the movie trailer and not the whole movie." A one-on-one plan should be conversational, with you being careful not to explain or talk too much. Overtalkers have a hard time sponsoring anyone into their business. So be mindful of the time and hit only the most important parts.

Activity, Part Two

For house plans in particular: For a house plan, it will not be possible to show up and have this type of leading conversation with all of the prospects in attendance, as you would for a one-on-one. Instead, when arriving at a house plan, have the host introduce you properly. You can then begin flipping through the flip chart and showing the plan. For a house plan, you will show more information and talk a bit more about each of the slides in the flip chart than you would be able to do during a one-on-one.

Your goal during the plan is to give the prospects a reason to delve into the materials you leave them and to attend an upcoming Open Meeting. Remember, hit the high points, be excited, find out what they really want in life, and get them to go through the *First Night Pack*. Keep it simple and reinforce to them how simple it is. Let them realize that they could easily do what you are doing.

The 8 Fs

The first part of the plan to cover, very briefly, is the concept of our "8 Fs." Simply let the prospect(s) know that the company you represent, LIFE Leadership, produces informational products designed to help people improve their lives in each of eight categories—the categories through which we find that people live out their lives. These are Faith, Family, Finances, Fitness, Following, Freedom, Friends, and Fun. You can explain that most people can stand to grow in at least one of these areas, if not several. This part of the plan is merely to frame the rest of the information you are going to present in its proper context. There is no need to spend much time here. Just use this explanation as a way to get started and give the prospect(s) an overall view of what you're going to share.

ESBI

This is one of the most important parts of your presentation.

Let the prospect(s) know that the *E* stands for "Employee." The *S* stands for "Self-Employed." The *B* represents a "B-Type Business," and the *I* refers to "Investors." According to author

Robert Kiyosaki, these represent the four main ways to make money. Briefly explain each of these categories.

Show that on the left side of the quadrant, 95 percent of the people are fighting over 5 percent of the money, whereas on the right side, it is exactly the opposite. You can relate your own story at this point, assuming you began your financial life somewhere on the left side of the quadrant like the rest of us. Tell them about how you felt stuck in a rut (if you did, of course) or whatever it was about your previous financial life that made you decide to get involved with LIFE Leadership. The point here is to help the prospect(s) understand that they are *not* doing "pretty well" or "pretty good." This part of the plan should help people break out of their comas of complacency. Note: It is important that you use your *own* situation on the left side of the quadrant to show the downside of living on that side and earning money in those ways. Never use the prospect(s) or their occupations as a negative example. The general principle is: Put all bad stuff on yourself. Put all good stuff on the prospect(s). For example, you might say, "Bob, you're probably doing pretty well in your job as a dentist. But as for me, I couldn't stand going in to my engineering job day after day knowing how much I would make in a year before the year even began." In this way, you help relate the futility of the left side of the quadrant without insulting the prospect(s) or what they do for a living.

This is also the section of the plan in which you relate the difference between trading time for money in a job or self-employed situation (E and S) and developing ongoing, residual income by investing time into something that brings a long-term return, such as investing or a B-type business (B and I). One way to do this is to describe the difference between carrying buckets (representing the left side of the quadrant) vs. building a pipeline (representing the right side of the quadrant). For more on these concepts, pick up a copy of *The Cashflow Quadrant* by Robert Kiyosaki and the first-night book *LIFE Leadership* (available on the lifeleadership.com Shopping Center).

It is a good idea to sprinkle the dream throughout this section of the plan. Talking about developing ongoing incomes and freeing up time is a likely spot for you to ask the prospect(s) what they would do with extra time or a background pipeline income. This sort of thing can be done throughout the entire plan, of course, but in this section, it is particularly effective.

Remember, the whole purpose of explaining the Cashflow Quadrant is to help the prospect(s) understand that they probably have needs either in the time department or with respect to income. Most people, if honest, would admit to a need for more of both!

Want Circle vs. Income Circle

This is an ideal time to refer to the concept of a Want Circle. You can explain that most people in life have a Want Circle that represents all their goals, dreams, and hopes for their life. At the same time, they are faced with an Income Circle (or Reality Circle). In the vast majority of cases, the two circles bear no resemblance to each other. Our Want Circles are usually enormous, and our Income Circles are often paltry by comparison.

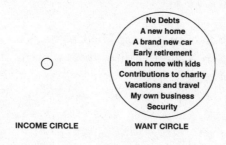

No Debts
A new home
A brand new car
Early retirement
Mom home with kids
Contributions to charity
Vacations and travel
My own business
Security

INCOME CIRCLE   WANT CIRCLE

In one-on-ones and in smaller groups, it is effective to ask the prospect(s) what they would have in their Want Circle that is beyond what they can get doing what they are currently doing. This is where the conversation at the beginning of the plan can come in helpful because by now, you know something about them. You may have noticed hobbies or sports in which they are interested and can refer back to those. Ask questions, listen intently, and try to find their "hot button." A very important part of what we do is find out what people truly desire deep in their hearts and then show them a way to get it using LIFE Leadership. Don't rush past this part of the plan. Find ways to get them thinking about the possibilities. It may be helpful to make some suggestions, such as time, travel, homes, cars, toys, charities, helping family members, getting out of debt, etc. (This will especially be necessary for house plans where you won't be able to discuss individual dreams.) If you can get the prospect(s) talking at this part of the plan, you will be well on your way to helping them see why this business makes sense for them. Remember, we are not in the business of getting people to do something. We are in the business of helping them get their dreams. If you don't discover what the prospect(s) really want, you are without leverage to help them do the things necessary to succeed.

When you find out what the prospect(s) really desire, let them know you are sincere about helping with the achievement of those dreams. As one of our team leaders says, "Bob, I'm the guy that's going to help you get that!" Your sincerity will likely catch them off guard, and your belief will instill in them the confidence that maybe, just maybe, it is not too late for them to still get their goals and dreams.

Michael Dell's 3 Cs

The next portion of the plan is Michael Dell's 3 Cs. The purpose of this section is to relate the three most important aspects of being in business in today's Information Age, as explained by legendary founder of Dell Computer Corporation, Michael Dell.

Activity, Part Two

It is best to give an overall, but quick, explanation of the slide. The point to make is that one of the geniuses who were part of ushering in the Information Age (Michael Dell) related that the new rules of success in the world would follow these "3 Cs." First, explain the Content slide, giving a brief overview of the point of the slide, and then turn to the next couple of slides that support it.

Content: Explain that this C represents the LIFE Leadership products. This is where it might be appropriate to talk about the bestselling status of the authors of this material and other third-party notoriety that validates the worth of the LIFE Leadership materials in the marketplace. **Remember to tell your prospect(s) that our product is *life-changing information* designed to help them live the life they've always wanted**. That is the key point of the Content C. Use the next couple of slides to support your explanation of this first C. One slide further into the flip chart is a slide depicting an arrangement of LIFE Leadership materials, followed by one explaining the 3 for FREE customer referral program. These are to be used in support of the first of Dell's 3 Cs: Content.

Next explain *Commerce:* This is where you discuss the overall concept of "where the money comes from" for those who become LIFE Members. Explain the difference between two arrangements of boxes depicting distribution systems. One represents the conventional, old-fashioned distribution system that includes lots of middlemen who eat up profits. The other represents an Information-Age distribution system that eliminates the middlemen, thereby freeing up those monies to be shared as profits in the LIFE Compensation Plan. Instead of the middlemen making the money on our transactions, the founders of LIFE Leadership have put together a pay plan to reward that money to those who merchandise LIFE Leadership products.

A helpful illustration of this is what the authors of this book experienced when our first book was sold to a big publishing firm. Formerly, we had published the book ourselves and therefore were able to keep those profits and use them to fund our charity, All Grace Outreach. Once the rights were sold to a third party, a complicated process ensued in which the profits were split among a whole host of participants. While this led to a wider audience for the book (for which we were thankful), it did illustrate very clearly to us that, from strictly a financial standpoint, certain arrangements in distribution are more profitable than others.

So with LIFE Leadership, we eliminate those middle costs and make that money available through a pay plan. How that money is sliced up and paid out in bonuses can be briefly explained using the next slide, titled "Compensated Community." It has a place on the left-hand side where you can describe Team Approach, our master strategy for building the business that helps everyone work together to build teams. The point to explain here is that the prospect(s) won't have to do all the work by themselves. Instead, they will be part of a team all working together to build a community. The right side of this slide has green boxes depicting three scenarios used to describe incomes. These are merely examples. Check with your upline support team to find out what numbers should be shown in these boxes. Also, be sure at this point to refer the prospect(s) to the "LIFE Leadership Compensation Plan and Income Disclosure Statement" brochure.

It is appropriate at this point to also introduce the concept of paid incentive trips, in particular, our 6,000 for 6 Incentive Trip. As the name suggests, these are paid trips to select resort locations made available to LIFE Members who build their businesses to certain levels. What is striking about these trips is not only the exciting vacation destinations involved but more so the low levels of business achievement required to earn them. Many companies in many industries make extravagant trips available to top officials and performers. That is nothing new. But LIFE Leadership wanted to turn that on its head. Instead, we provide dream vacations (you get to choose from several options) for LIFE Members who are on the earlier side of their business journey. We figure that once you have built a huge business, you will be interested in paying for your own trips. But during the earlier days of your business experience, you are more likely to appreciate and feel inspired by a mind-blowing trip. Therefore, we have rolled out some of the best, most exciting getaways imaginable, all achievable in your first year or so of the business.

Activity, Part Two

The next of Michael Dell's 3 Cs is ***Community***. The slide used to explain it is labeled "Community: Value of LIFE Training System." This one depicts the importance of community building and highlights the LIFE Training materials that support this activity. This is to let the prospect(s) know that they may be in business *for* themselves, but they will not be *by* themselves. A helpful illustration of community might be the wild enthusiasm of Pittsburg Steelers fans worldwide or the passionate following Apple Computer Corporation has amassed. These are illustrations of exactly what happens when the customer is *beyond* satisfied and instead becomes downright jubilant. It is this kind of excitement that usually follows the improvement of people's lives once they have been positiviely influenced by the LIFE Leadership materials and/or community.

At the end of your presentation, the assignment that you should give is for the prospect(s) to listen to the first-night audios and go through the *LIFE Leadership* book (which we've been calling the "first-night book") and any of the other first-night materials, such as brochures and pamphlets. Promote them to the prospect(s) in detail at this point, specifically tying the information in these materials to their dreams. Give some background on the speakers featured in the talks, and explain why they will want to listen. Show them how the book will answer most of their questions, and encourage them to read through it. Show them the pictures and comics inside, and let them know that it is easy reading!

Handling Objections during the Plan

To help increase your effectiveness, it is sometimes helpful to handle common objections during the course of your plan. For example, if you seem to consistently receive the same question or objection when you show the plan, begin handling that objection in your plan before your prospect(s) can raise it themselves. Below are commonly heard examples of objections you may encounter repeatedly and will want to learn how to handle in advance.

Is This a Pyramid?

To prevent this objection, you could explain a little about illegal pyramid schemes and then how LIFE Leadership differs. Factors that may constitute an illegal pyramid are:

- Up-front product loading
- Making money by recruiting
- No retail customers
- Those who get in first having a different financial arrangement than those who get in later

Explain that LIFE Leadership doesn't have or allow product loading or incomes generated by recruiting others to join and that we have retail customer requirements. Also, anybody can make more than anybody else, regardless of when or where the individuals came into the business. The money doesn't go to those who got in first.

Contrast these notions of a pyramid with the *Team Approach* method of building communities. This may be done most effectively when explaining the pay plan and describing the bonus chart. Let the prospect(s) know that they can earn more money than the person who invited them into the business, based upon performance.

They've Seen This Kind of Thing Before

Explain that what LIFE Leadership is doing has really never been done before. The founders of the company have decades and decades of experience in this profession. They had come to learn the best and the worst of what the industry was doing and founded LIFE Leadership to fix all the problems and challenges they'd experienced in their past with other companies. As they like to say, they didn't found LIFE Leadership to *make* a lot of money; they founded it to *pay* a lot of money. LIFE Leadership is not simply another networking company. It is one that is turning the industry around!

Activity, Part Two

At the Close of the Plan

Now let's get back to the process of showing the plan. To close the plan, take a couple minutes to go back to the prospects' dreams and remind them to quit waiting for their ship to come in. If they want better health, we have a plan for that. If they want to make some money, we have a plan for that. If they want both, we have a plan for that, too. In fact, LIFE Leadership has a plan for an improved life in *all* of the 8 F categories!

For house plans in particular: If your spouse is involved, introduce him or her at this point (that is, at the end of the main presentation). The enthusiasm of the spouses (where applicable) is extremely important. Your spouse can express how strongly he or she believes in what you just shared and the future of LIFE Leadership.

After the plan (and after your spouse's comments if applicable), the host of the meeting should be brought forward to share some closing comments. The objective here is for the host to reiterate how excited he or she is about the business and to express commitment to building it. This is also a great opportunity to compliment the speaker on a job well done. Appropriate closing remarks are short and enthusiastic. A possible example might be: "Now you can all see why (spouse) and I are so excited! (Speaker) did a great job of explaining it, and we appreciate him (or her) coming tonight. We have decided to move ahead in LIFE Leadership full speed, and we are delighted that you've had a chance to see what we are so excited about. We would love to work with you if you determine it's for you, too! We have some materials to leave with you, and we can take some time individually to answer any questions you may have. Also, (plan presenter) has agreed to stick around to help answer any questions and to teach us how to get started fast." These comments, or something very similar, are the most appropriate. **It is not appropriate to thank the audience for coming.** If they understand the value of what they just saw, they will thank the host for inviting them! **Also, it is not appropriate to open the meeting up for questions and answers at the end.** Break up the meeting, get the crowd into the kitchen or some other mingling spot, and let questions be addressed individually.

The presenter of the house plan should then mingle, picking out the most excited prospects, giving them first-night materials, booking individual follow-through appointments, and/or signing up new customers and LIFE Members (described in more detail below). The host and any other upline present should do the same things with the other prospects.

For both house plans and one-on-ones: Tell the prospect(s) why you think they would be good at the business, and let them know you would like to work with them. If the prospect(s) are ready to get started, you can sign them up at the close of the plan. Your goal is to either sign people up or, at a minimum, sign a pre-application with no credit card information included. If any of the prospects are a "maybe" and want to do their homework assignments by going through the materials you recommended before taking any action, then a pre-application is perfect for them. You simply record on the form (registration forms, which can also be used as pre-registration forms, are downloadable for free from lifeleadership.com) the date and time that you showed them the plan and tell them that anyone you or your teammates show the plan to after this time could potentially end up on *their* team. This represents no commitment to sign up, but it gives you all of their information for when you get the next "Yes" and call them back.

This process is referred to as a "squeeze." It involves calling someone back (or going back to that person's house) once other prospects on that same team have agreed to join. Chronologically speaking, if you showed Prospect A the plan before someone on the team (or you yourself) showed Prospect B, it is only fair to ask Prospect A if he or she would now like to get in and therefore have Prospect B on his or her team. All you are doing is giving Prospect A one final chance to have the teammates on his or her team that he or she *would have had* if he or she had signed up the moment you showed him or her the plan. It might be helpful to tell Prospect A something like, "It might not be clear to you why it is an advantage to have people you don't know yet on your team, *but you'll thank me later!*"

Whether people sign up immediately or not, you should expect to pass out first-night materials like crazy at the end of the plan. If you don't have these materials on hand and ready to pass out, you are out of business! Give them a hunger for diving into the materials you have recommended during the plan. Promote each of the materials and create the hunger for the prospect(s) to review them. Just handing them out is not enough. You must put an emphasis on the materials that will make the prospect(s) *want* to review them.

Next, take out your calendar and schedule a time to get back together with the prospect(s) or new sign-up(s) and answer any of their questions. Tell them that tonight you have explained what the business is, and when you get back together, you will cover the *how* side of actually building it and getting them started properly toward realizing their dreams. The best time to get back together for the follow-through is within two days. Any longer than that, and the prospect(s) may tend to lose interest. As the saying goes, "Time kills all interest." Do not leave the house without booking a follow-through appointment! **The plan presenter should never leave without booking a follow-through.**

Also, after booking the follow-through, it is appropriate to invite the prospect(s) to the next Open Meeting. It is usually a good idea to offer to pick them up and take them to the Open. They are more likely to come if you bring them. Please note: It is best to book a follow-through even when the prospect(s) are planning to attend the Open Meeting. The two are very different activities, and if the prospect(s) miss the Open, you are forced to call and "chase" them down, as we discussed before. To avoid this issue, simply book the follow-through first and then arrange to have them attend the Open Meeting.

There is a natural tendency to feel good at the end of showing a plan, and it is tempting to skip the final touches that make it all worthwhile. Resist that temptation. Be a professional and complete the job thoroughly and properly. Also, some people have a tendency to overstay their welcome. Although there is a lot going on, especially at a successful house plan, it is not advisable to stay too long talking to everyone afterward. The best time to leave is just a moment or two before people want you to! Understanding when that is becomes a matter of discretion that you will grow more sensitive to as you perfect this process. Play it safe, however, not hurrying out of there like you don't care but being careful not to overstay your welcome either!

One final note: There is an optional feature available to subscribers to the LIFE Training Marketing System called "Branded Emails." These are graphically pleasing, professionally constructed email templates that allow you to attach an amazing amount of information with a simple click. Perhaps a prospect showed interest in a particular category of materials, one of the 8 Fs, for instance. In that case, immediately after showing him or her the plan, you could send an email with links to several relevant articles, video clips, or other pieces of information from the website, stating, "I think this is some of the information you wanted" or "I think this information will help answer your questions." This becomes an easy way to provide a plethora of information and help the prospect satisfy his or her natural desire to do research on what you presented.

Keep It Simple

We have covered a lot in this section regarding both the principles and the specifics of showing the plan. The purpose of a book like this is to be as comprehensive as possible, providing as much information as we can to assist you, the LIFE Member, in growing your business fast and profitably. In that spirit, we have tried to include as much here as we could without making it too overwhelming.

Perhaps we have failed. The danger in attempting to be complete and thorough is that things can begin to seem complicated and difficult. This is not the case with showing the plan and sharing the awesome LIFE Leadership materials. It should be easy, simple, and fun. We have thrown all these details in to make sure you have adequate information to work toward mastery. However, even the newest LIFE Member can experience tremendous success showing the plan and sharing the materials. It's really as easy as flipping through the flip chart or scribbling on the sketchpad. If you can do these simple steps, you can build this business! The key is to keep it simple, have fun, and show it enough to get good at it and have the law of averages working in your favor. That brings us to the next topic: Go-Getter!

Go-Getter

We have gone through the details of showing the plan. Now let's talk a little bit about the pace of the business, in other words, how often one shows the plan.

The Power Player Program states that Power Players show the plan themselves fifteen times or more per month. This is a very critical activity level that has been proven over and over again. It is okay to start slower than that and ramp up, but understand the importance of working up to a level of activity that allows your business a chance to gain momentum and prosper. Showing fifteen plans per month can be compared to treading water. There is a certain amount of arm and leg strokes that keep the swimmer afloat; anything less, even a *little* less, and the swimmer is not a swimmer for long! Showing fifteen plans a month works much the same way. It is a level of activity that not only keeps the business owner's business afloat but also propels it forward. Less than that on a consistent basis will lead to some sinking. Go-Getters are recognized onstage at the Monthly Seminars. All Power Players hit the Go-Getter level on a regular, monthly basis.

Summary

For your business to grow, it will be necessary to become adept at showing the plan yourself. In the beginning, your upline will show plans on your behalf. This is to help you get started growing a business and to demonstrate how it is done. Your job will be to introduce people to the LIFE Leadership materials and business so your upline can come in and help you. Eventually, you will take over showing plans to grow your own business. The good news is that this is one of the most fascinating and enjoyable steps in the entire business. People are infinitely interesting and therefore fun to meet and get to know. And as you show the plan, you will collect relationships and stories that will warm your heart, make you laugh, and build a big business.

The only thing necessary for the triumph of evil is for good men to do nothing.
—Unknown (sometimes attributed to Edmund Burke)

It is not enough to be industrious; so are the ants. What are you industrious about?
—Henry David Thoreau

Don't worry about whether you're better than somebody else, but never cease trying to be the best you can become. You have control over that; the other you don't.
—John Wooden

Everything comes to him who hustles while he waits.
—Thomas Edison

I can accept failure; everyone fails at something. But I can't accept not trying.
—Michael Jordan

Name: NEGATIVE NANCY
Quote: "How much money are you making? You know all those things are scams. My uncle's doctor's daughter got into one of those things, and she lost everything."

CHAPTER 7

ACTIVITY, PART THREE
FOLLOWING THROUGH AND GETTING
THEM STARTED (ROTATING THE PATTERN)

After showing the plan, the remaining steps in the Five-Step Pattern are:

4. Following Through
5. Getting Them Started (Rotating the Pattern)

In the Information Age, the battleground is in each of our minds. Those with the correct information win. Those without it, for instance, those stuck in Industrial-Age thinking, lose. Therefore, it is of the utmost importance to involve all new potential business owners in the LIFE Training system as soon as possible. It is like being sure a horse dying of thirst gets to water quickly. There will be enough time later for attending to the details of bridles and saddles. Signing up a new business owner is a bridle and saddle activity. It is surely important, but only after the horse is nourished. Getting people involved with the LIFE Leadership materials and the system is the water.

Following Through

We begin this chapter with a discussion about getting prospective LIFE Members in motion and leading them to the LIFE Training Marketing System because that is exactly what the follow-through step is really all about. To learn more about this part of the process, be sure to consult the many audios that teach this topic in detail. The main components of *following through* are:

1. Refamiliarize them with their dream.
2. Answer questions.

3. Overcome objections.
4. Involve them in the system.
5. Begin rotating the pattern on their behalf.
6. Continue building a relationship.

Refamiliarize Them with Their Dream

Between the plan and the follow-through, many things can happen. Usually, the prospective LIFE Member(s) have asked other people for their opinions about the business. While it should be obvious that those *uninvolved* with the business and most likely *not financially successful* are not valuable sources of assessment, it is a natural tendency for all of us to bounce ideas off people we know. As a result, the prospective business owner(s) might have received negative feedback. Simply be prepared to handle it. The best way to do this is to be thoroughly involved in the LIFE Training Marketing System yourself so that you have the information to counter any misconceptions that may be out there. Then, understand that nobody really wants to *do* the business; the only reason anybody gets involved is for what they can *accomplish through* the "doing" of the business. Nobody wants something else to *do*; what they want is a better lifestyle. Obviously, your business is one of the best ways to accomplish a better lifestyle, and that is what should be emphasized during the follow-through step. This is what we call refamiliarizing them with their dream.

Specifically, it is a good idea to draw out a circle on a piece of paper and ask the prospective business owner(s) to refresh your memory as to what they would like to achieve in the next two to five years if money and time were not an object. This step is designed to get them focused on the dream again. Remember, the only reason people get involved in your business is "what's in it for them." It is critical at the follow-through step to drive this point home. We quoted Carl Sandburg in chapter one as saying, "Nothing happens without first a dream." It is of primary importance to help the prospect(s) remember that the whole thing they are considering when looking at your business is whether or not they really want their dreams. Let's face it; without a proper vehicle, most people will not attain the majority of their goals and dreams. As one man said, "They will die with their music still in them." Therefore, the question isn't "Do you want to participate in my business?" but rather "Do you want your dreams?" Your business simply plugs people into a way to get their dreams. The analogy is the purchasing of a power drill. Does the buyer really want a drill, or does he or she want a hole? The drill is simply a tool to provide the end result the buyer actually desires. Your business is like the drill.

Answer Questions

The most natural thing that will happen at a follow-through is for the prospective business owner(s) to have some questions. Be sure and spend the time required to help the prospect(s) understand your business by providing the best information you can. This is why it is so important to be involved in the LIFE Training Marketing System and familiar with the LIFE Leadership products yourself so that you will have the answers and the confidence to provide those answers.

However, the very best way to answer questions is by using the LIFE Training system itself. Instead of answering every question yourself, allow the system to do it. What do we mean by this? Well, what if someone asks a question regarding the legality of the business? A correct way to answer this would be to give them a copy of one of the audios in the system that addresses that very question. You could even promote the audio by saying, "Here's my brief version of the answer to that question, but I'm no lawyer. In this talk right here, a very distinguished lawyer gives his analysis of our business. It has a lot more detail than I could give you. The answer to your question is in this talk." In this way, you become the *messenger* and not the *message*. You become a doorway to the information instead of the source of the information itself. The most effective business owners understand that they must rely on the system in such a way.

Overcome Objections

People sometimes get hung up on what they should do or say when prospective business owners have objections of some kind. The first thing to realize is that objections to something new are quite normal. If you think back, you probably had an objection or two to getting involved in many things about which you later became enthusiastic. The difference was information and experience. Considered in this way, objections may even be a sign of sincere interest in learning more about your business. After all, nobody takes the time to offer up objections for something in which he or she has absolutely no interest. If a person has absolutely no interest in a subject, he or she simply says, "No."

There is a difference, however, between an objection and an excuse. An objection is a legitimate concern, which, if properly addressed, will go away and clear the path for progress. An excuse is an annoying little thing, which, if addressed, will only give birth to another. That is how you can tell the difference between a sincere objection and an excuse.

Author Frank Bettger wrote about a way to distinguish between an objection and an excuse. Instead of addressing an objection (or excuse) head on, Bettger said to simply ask the question, "Besides that, would there be anything *else* that would hold you back?" If the reply is another reason, then the first reason offered was not really an objection but an excuse. This could continue through several excuses. Finally, by repeatedly asking that same question, you will arrive at a point where there are no more excuses. The *last* thing holding up the prospect is the real objection. All others before that were simply excuses.

Larry VanBuskirk has another way of accomplishing the same thing. His question is, "Oh really, why is that?" (It should be noted, however, that Larry claims this is much more effective if pronounced as we will spell it here phonetically: "OREALLY WHYZAT?") Repeating this question a few times ought to drive at the real reason.

Use either approach. The goal is to get to the real objection so time can be spent finding a real solution or work-around instead of wasted chopping away at fake excuses.

Another good way to deal with objections, because many are just fears or lack of information, is to follow the formula of Feel, Felt, and Found. If you are offered an objection for which the statement rings true, you can respond with, "I know how you *feel*. I *felt* the same way, but here's what I *found*...." Again, make sure you are sincere, and don't use this simply as some type of tactic on someone. But if you truly did feel that way, empathize with their position first; then let them know what information or perspective was helpful to you in getting past the objection. However, be careful not to be cheesy with this idea. Remember, authenticity and sincerity are what truly matter in human relations, not techniques and cute phrases.

As you gain experience building your business, you will discover that of all the people you will run across, most share the same two or three concerns about getting started. The problem, eventually, will *not* be that you don't know the answer but, rather, that you have to decide how to choose from the *too many* pieces of information you could give in reply!

Involve Them in the System

We have been making this point over and over: The goal of these early moments in the experience of new business owners is to lead them to the information that has the potential to help them get their dreams. Each step of the way, this is accomplished through audios, books, pamphlets, and involvement in meetings.

At the follow-through appointment, invitations should be made to the next Open Meeting, and more informational materials should be left for review. **It is critical to get them to the next Open Meeting** so they can meet the community, get more information, and begin to get a bigger picture of what you are doing. Also, be sure to promote each piece of material you loan out by explaining its specific relevance to their situation. "You will love this talk; it's by a husband and wife who were both teachers, just like you two" or "This book goes through the exact details it takes to build your leadership skills, just like you were asking." You have to create a hunger on the part of your prospect(s) to delve deeper into the information.

Another way to do this, as we explained in the section on showing the plan, is to tie things back to the dream. For instance, you might encounter some who are hesitant to invest the time or money to attend an upcoming seminar. You must help them see the *value* in attending. Remember to always help them see "what's in it for them." Your promotion of the event might go like this: "Bob, I know you wanted more detailed information on how to build your community, and this upcoming seminar is going to provide just that. At the event, they'll lay out all the information in a format that makes it easy to learn, and you'll come out of there with a much clearer idea of how to build your business. I think you'll be able to see how you might be able to afford that log cabin you want to build." The key is this: Don't ever try to *get* people to *do* anything. Try to help them get what they want by encouraging them to do what is necessary. LIFE Members are sort of like a "Merit" Santa Claus; they give people a way to get what they want.

Begin Rotating the Pattern on Their Behalf

The reason we call this step in the pattern "follow-through" instead of "follow-up" is because we are most interested in continuing the process before it's even really begun. This may sound confusing, but allow us to explain.

We could go through all the work of trying to help others become convinced to participate as business owners, get them "signed up," etc. We could spend hours and hours answering their questions. But a much more effective way to help them get a feel for the business is for them to simply give it a try. It's a lot like a new car dealership allowing prospective customers to test drive a new vehicle to help them decide whether to purchase it. We can easily help them share the product (life-changing information) and/or show the plan, even before they are officially business owners themselves.

Many times, upon seeing the plan, people become excited. They begin thinking of people with whom they'd like to share the idea and/or information. Remember as we said before, it is natural for people to want to go out and solicit opinions about the business anyway. Why not do it the *correct way*? Why not have them go out and solicit opinions *with you*, someone who can show the plan and help them? In this way, it goes from a function of collecting opinions to a process of sharing the plan and/or product with more people. This process can begin as soon as you are done showing the plan. You can suggest that the idea could be bounced off some other people immediately, depending on the prospect's schedule. "How's right now?" you might ask. Sometimes this works; sometimes it doesn't. But it doesn't hurt to ask. If the prospect(s) can't or won't lead you to anybody else immediately, sometimes they *can* by the next day or so. Great. This initiates the Five-Step Pattern all over again and effectively becomes what we term "building depth," which is a concept we'll highlight in chapter eight.

Sometimes, however, the prospective new business owner(s) are not ready to begin talking to their friends right away. In those instances, you should conduct the follow-through by initiating the Five-Step Pattern on their behalf. After you have answered their questions, loaned them more training materials, and promoted and invited them to the next meeting, you can begin helping them with step one (generating a list of names). This does not have to be an exhaustive exercise, but it is normally liberating for the prospect(s). This is because with the help of a memory jogger pamphlet, the "Who Do You Know?" brochure (TL242), the prospect(s) can rather quickly generate a large list of names. This becomes exciting for them as they realize they know a lot of people. By helping them take the first step, you are also gently walking them into the business by showing them that they can do the activity and that you will be there to assist them.

Depending on how well the making of the names list goes, you can next encourage the prospect(s) to move to step two of the Five-Step Pattern and contact a few people on the list. This takes us back to what we were doing above when we decided to just show the plan to the people the prospect(s) would solicit opinions from anyway. At this point, you are trying to get the prospect(s) to make a formal appointment with those on their names list, or perhaps you are trying to help the prospect(s) make contacts by getting out and sharing the LIFE Leadership materials. It is crucial to assist them on this step, although many will say they'd rather do it alone later. Either way, be sure to prep them on at least the basic principles of contacting before they begin, but don't overwhelm or "over train" them.

Helping the prospect(s) take these initial steps of the Five-Step Pattern may not happen all at one meeting. It may take several visits to get them moving through these steps. For instance, you might answer their questions and leave them some more materials at the first follow-through appointment. Then they attend an Open Meeting, and you get back together the next day. **Always remember to book a meeting from a meeting.** Now they are ready to make their names list but not ready to contact anybody yet. Give them some more materials and pick another time to get back with them. At that stage, it will likely be time to begin contacting and scheduling their first house plan. All of this is okay. As long as they are showing sincere interest and not just wasting your time, allow the process to move along at a pace that is at least a little comfortable for them. However, your time is valuable, too. And it is all a balance. You don't want to be rushing the process along at such a pace that they feel overwhelmed or "pushed" into doing anything. On the other hand, you can't make trip after trip to meet with prospect(s) that aren't really taking action in the business. In each case, this will be a judgment call on your part. The trick is to get your calendar as full as you want it with appointments with other people so that you really only have time for those who are the hungriest.

Remember, the hungriest people in life are the ones that succeed the biggest, and that's exactly who we are looking for through this whole process. So don't push people too fast, but don't let them waste your time (or theirs) either.

Continue Building a Relationship

This industry is built on relationships. In fact, most businesses are; that's what Michael Dell meant by "building communities." But perhaps no business category runs on relationships as much as LIFE Leadership. For that reason, it is vitally important to always remember that relationships are more important than tasks. We should never get so caught up in the Five-Step Pattern or the objectives of what we are trying to accomplish in the follow-through step or promoting the next seminar or any other task that we lose site of the *relationships*. People come before tasks. They are the most important part of your business and, for that matter, the most important part of life. As the saying goes, "We are here to serve other people."

We discussed building relationships in the section on showing the plan. The principles are exactly the same for the follow-through step. Take an interest in the other person(s). Learn to listen, and by all means, do not be an overtalker. Be sincere. Try to find common ground. Be real, open, and honest. In short, become a friend.

Every step of your business (from the initial contact to showing the plan, following through, attending events, and making phone calls) is an opportunity for building a tighter relationship with those with whom you are building your business. Take every activity in your business as a chance to build a tighter bond with people. As one successful business owner once said, "I try to go around sprinkling a little bit of sunshine everywhere I go."

Signing Them Up

We talked quite a bit about signing up new Members in the last chapter on showing the plan. It may be helpful to discuss it a little further at this point, going into some of the philosophies and thought processes behind the right way to do it.

Some people sign up right away; others sign up later. Whether prospect(s) sign up immediately or not is up to them. But the part that is up to you, the one who shows the plan, is to ask for their commitment. In other words, ask them to join your team. There is usually an increase in commitment to something once somebody has committed some of his or her money to it. For that reason, it matters that the prospect(s) eventually *do* sign up.

The best way to get this to happen is to ask for it. At the end of the plan, once the initial questions have been answered, you might say, "So are you guys ready to hold your spot on the team?" or "I'd love to have you guys on board with us. Are you ready to become official as LIFE Members?" or "I think we've got a good match here. Can I officially welcome you to my team (extending your hand across the table for a handshake)?" Another approach Tim Marks has popularized is, "Do you want to know why most people I show this to join this on the spot? (Pause) It's because there is little or no risk; the product is something that will improve their lives, and you can do as little or as much as you want." For more leverage and fast growth, discuss the "first mover advantage," where a new enrollee who gets in ahead of those that come later is in a position to benefit from that business volume.

Whichever of these methods you use to ask the prospect(s) to enroll, your next step (and this is the toughest part) is to sit quietly and let them decide. Don't fill the air with words. Wait for their reply. If their answer is "No, not yet," you can dig into their reason why. (See the section a few pages back entitled "Overcoming Objections.") If you can't turn around their objections (and don't push too hard here; remember, signing them up is not the main objective), then just say "Great" and continue with the process of leaving materials and booking the follow-through (or next follow-through). This is also when you would have them fill out the pre-registration form we talked about earlier, which will enable you to call back later with a "squeeze play." (See chapter six.) If it is "Yes," then just say "Great" and pull out the LIFE Leadership registration form for them to fill out.

Ask your upline for the specifics about the sign-up package and what it includes, as having everyone sign up the same way with the same materials is a duplicatable, repeatable process that becomes an important building block in your business. In LIFE Leadership, we like to model the principles of franchising. One of the biggest principles that has made franchises successful is the concept that "Discretion is the enemy of duplication." When there is discretion (in other words, an abundance of choices and differing strategies and actions), it creates confusion and slow growth. When everyone does the process the same, duplication and multiplication result, and the business can grow fast. One of the most important places for this is right at the beginning when you are signing up a brand new LIFE Member. Do it right and allow the power of duplication to work for you!

Preventing Overload

Guard yourself against giving people drinks of water through a fire hose. It is sometimes a tendency among LIFE Members to overwhelm prospects with too much information. The important principle to remember is "What's Important Next?" There are many, many great pieces of information to tell prospects about your business, but all in due time. Be careful to focus only on what is vital for their success at that point in the journey. The prospects or new LIFE Members can learn all about the details of various elements later as they become more familiar with their new venture. It is your job to help them concentrate on the one or two most important things to do next and prevent overload. You will only be able to do this if you become capable of "reading" people a little bit. Learn to look for the signs of disinterest or fatigue. Look for indications that certain things excite them more than others. Again, as with so many aspects of this industry, the better you know people and how to deal with them, the better off you'll be.

Getting Them Started (Rotating the Pattern)

Rotating the pattern has really already been discussed. If you do step four (following through) properly, you will begin initiating the new LIFE Member(s) in the process of exposing new people to the business. By helping them make a list, contact people, show the plan, and follow through with those people, you are helping *them* rotate the pattern and, in fact, doing the fifth step of the pattern!

Guess what you do when the prospect(s) or new LIFE Member(s) lead you to some people who have dreams and are looking? Exactly the same thing. Now you help them rotate the pattern to find the people *they* know who are looking. This is really the beginning of the concept called "building depth," which we will discuss in the next chapter.

But let's say that you do all the steps in the process properly, and someone still isn't interested in getting involved as a LIFE Member. Now what do you do? We like to help Members understand that when you rotate this pattern, at the end of it, only two things will happen:

1. You get a new business partner on your team.
2. You get a new customer.

If it turns out that the business isn't for a particular prospect (because as we like to say, although everyone has a life, this LIFE isn't for *everyone*), then the next step should be to turn him or her into a customer. You have spent at least a little time with this prospect. You have built rapport with him or her (hopefully). You have started a relationship, or perhaps already had one. Making him or her a customer is a natural next step. (And in the case of certain styles of contacting, you made him or her a customer immediately upon sharing the materials with him or her in the initial exposure.) People sometimes ask us, "Where and how do I find my customers?" One way is through the efforts you are expending toward building your community. You've invested time and energy in this prospect; now finish it off with some customer volume. Doing so is also a great way to stay in touch with a person and to keep him or her thinking about your business, and it provides a window into your forthcoming success. Often, people say "No" to a business and simply become customers at first. And then later, they get interested in LIFE Membership because of what they see changing in the life of the person who showed them the plan. Also, other people can take an interest in the products they see those customer(s) using, and this helps show the customer(s) that the business could work for them!

In fact, the 3 for FREE Program allows a customer to sign up three other customers (using his or her customer number) to monthly subscriptions to the LIFE Leadership materials. Once a customer has signed up three other subscribing customers on equivalent dollar value subscriptions, his or her LIFE Leadership subscription will be free the next month. This exciting program applies to all customers and LIFE Members! This just might bring an amazed LIFE Leadership customer back to you as a business partner someday down the road.

Even more to the point, your business ultimately comes down to monthly product flow. Even though a big part of the focus of this book is on the *community building* aspect of LIFE Leadership, obviously an enormous component is *customer volume*. Remember, you are building a community through which life-changing information flows. The more customer volume a new Member can generate, the sooner he or she will be profitable and the higher those profits will be. (Keep in mind that all LIFE Members receive 25 percent profit right off the top on every Registered Customer sale, no matter how new or how experienced they are in the business. This is an enormous margin!) So take advantage of the work you've already done in the Five-Step Pattern and learn to acquire customers. And don't forget to tell everyone about the 3 for FREE Program!

Don't stand shivering upon the bank; plunge in at once, and have it over with.
—Sam Glick

Work is much more fun than fun.
—Noël Coward

The harder I work, the luckier I get.
—Unknown (sometimes attributed to Thomas Jefferson)

The world is full of willing people, some willing to work, the rest willing to let them.
—Robert Frost

Some who are not paid what they are worth ought to be glad.
—Unknown

Name: NED THE KNOW-IT-ALL
Quote: "That's a neat little idea you
       got, but you're doing it all
       wrong. Let me tell you how
       to fix that so you can make
       some REAL money."

CHAPTER 8

RESULTS, PART ONE
BUILDING DEPTH

We have already covered a lot of ground in this book. We've discussed dreams and wealth thinking, introduced the overall concept of the Power Player Program, and talked through the theory and activity portions of the program. Now it is time to learn about *results*. We need to know what kind of results at which to aim and how to measure those results. Understanding theory is great. Doing the activity required for success is wonderful. But we must follow a specific strategy and then measure how we are doing to keep our business on track toward our goals and dreams.

The Theory of Depth

Every successful business enterprise must have a key strategy that makes everything work. Author Robert Kiyosaki calls it the "tactic that all strategies are based upon." Author Jim Collins calls it "the Hedgehog Concept." Name it what you will; the message is the same. In order to thrive, a business must have a core competency, an advantage that is utilized to accomplish success.

With the LIFE Training system, that core competency is the concept of teaching people how to "build depth." This is a deep subject (pun intended; we couldn't resist) but well worth digging into (sorry). Depth is the condition where one LIFE Member registers or signs up another LIFE Member into his or her business. In the business relationship that results, a bond is formed. As more bonds are formed and each new LIFE Member enrolls in the opportunity "under" the previous business owner, "depth" results. See the diagram that follows:

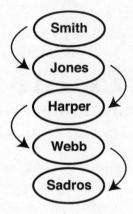

Depth accomplishes many things in the health of your organization. Included in these are:

1. Providing proof to new LIFE Members that this works
2. Building large numbers of people into your organization
3. Providing the best leverage for your time
4. Producing a secure business

Providing Proof to New LIFE Members That This Works

Depth is important for many reasons. One main reason is that people need a little proof that LIFE Leadership is real and that it actually works. As they see depth develop underneath them, they begin to believe that a large organization could be the result of continuing such growth. This increased belief increases their excitement, which normally increases their activity level, which increases the speed at which they do the work to grow their business, which increases their belief, etc. A simpler way of putting it is that **depth is the wedge that drives open the door of momentum.** Once depth begins happening consistently and quickly enough in an organization, that group takes off at astounding growth rates. People get excited, others join the organization at a furious rate, and the resulting product flow becomes enormous. This also, obviously, adds to the excitement and belief.

As we discussed before, if *information* gets a person interested in your business in the beginning, *progress* increases that interest. Building depth demonstrates progress. Finally, as the organization grows, *income* solidifies that interest into belief!

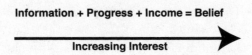

Building Large Numbers of People into Your Organization

Depth is the most effective method for building large numbers of people in a community. The deeper an organization becomes, the more exponential the growth of the numbers. To cause an explosion in the numbers of people involved in your business, **build depth** with a purpose, track it, and build it appropriately.

Providing the Best Leverage for Your Time

Depth also is a mighty form of time leveraging. Imagine an organization in which there was no depth but only something called "width." In such an organization, the leading member would have to "split" his or her time among each new participant. This is a division of time and effort and a dilution of energy, at best. One hour given assisting a new member results in one hour given. But with depth, an hour given to assist someone deep within an organization has the effect of helping everybody "above" that person in the organization. If you were to work in a location ten levels in depth below yourself and contribute an hour of your time, you would effectively gain ten hours worth of results! For this reason, the best businesses are the ones that actively encourage and reward the building of depth. Incidentally, the LIFE Leadership Compensation Plan (please see the brochure entitled "The LIFE Leadership Compensation Plan and Income Disclosure Statement") has many built-in rewards intentionally designed to reward the finding and developing of strong leaders *in depth*.

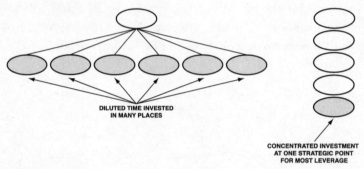

DILUTED TIME INVESTED
IN MANY PLACES

CONCENTRATED INVESTMENT
AT ONE STRATEGIC POINT
FOR MOST LEVERAGE

Producing a Secure Business

Depth also produces security. As an organization gets deeper and deeper, it has an increased ability to hold people together as a strong team. This is because so many people are in a position of potentially making money. With such a large group established "under" them, the potential for incomes becomes enormous. This is because of the sheer numbers involved. All that is required for someone with one deep organization to begin producing larger and larger incomes is to capitalize on the growth by duplicating that example in another, second organization.

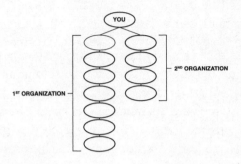

The Specifics of Depth

Understanding that depth is important and that it is the key to developing a large community of people through which life-changing information flows is one thing. Learning *how* to build it is another.

Building depth is not complicated. In fact, it is very simple. To do it, simply contact someone, show him or her the plan, and help him or her lead you to someone else to show the plan to; then repeat the process over and over again. We discussed this heavily in the previous chapter, but perhaps a diagram will be helpful.

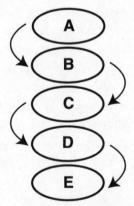

First, show the plan to Person (or Couple) A. As you follow the Five-Step Pattern in your dealings with Person A, he or she will lead you to Person B. Person B then leads you to Person C, and so on.

123

Team Approach

Team Approach is the name for the master strategy taught in the LIFE Training Marketing System. It can be seen in action when a group focuses on building depth at the bottom of an organization. The combined efforts of several LIFE Members helping everybody at the bottom grow the business "deeper" can result in faster growth and more momentum for everybody in the leg. This is because even if one LIFE Member doesn't achieve results in depth on a certain day, one of the other LIFE Members assisting in the bottom of the organization may.

Team Approach also involves the "squeeze play" that we discussed in chapters six and seven. By helping people understand that a team of people working together can grow a collective business to everyone's benefit, prospects are more likely to get in by "holding their spot" on the team. A squeeze is used to give a prospect one more chance to have the people on his or her team that he or she would have had anyway if he or she had signed up immediately upon seeing the plan.

There are a couple of angles to the squeeze play. The first one is during the plan when you explain to the prospect that he or she will get people on his or her team because you (and quite likely others in your upline) will be showing more plans to people who will go below the prospect's chronological position. One might call this a "forecasted" squeeze. Another aspect of the squeeze play is when you give a prospect a pre-application to fill out, thereby recording the date and time you showed him or her the plan. This allows you to come back later as described. A final aspect is when you and several partners in your team who all happen to be working in the same depth spot within an organization coordinate efforts and get together with all of your yeses, nos, and maybes. Considering the chronology, the nos and maybes can be contacted to see if they would like to get involved now that they have a team growing (should they sign up). This group approach is sometimes called a "squeeze group meeting" or a "squeeze board meeting."

The Team Approach results in faster growth than a lone individual could accomplish.

Apprenticeship Program

A key aspect to any successful training program is learning from those who have already experienced success. In getting started in the Power Player Program, as we've stated before, new LIFE Members will be in business *for* themselves but not *by* themselves. We call this, informally, an *apprenticeship program*. The concept of working with a team of people to build depth accomplishes this quite naturally. You will be working together with others on the team that you've joined to add new LIFE Members to the organization. In this way, not everyone "under" your position comes from you. Others will also be contributing to this same area of your business. It's a true team approach!

After a little progress in this area, you will naturally want to initiate your "second leg," or team, as well. The Power Player Program has a recommended strategy for when to begin constructing your second leg (while also continuing to grow your first leg).

When to Start Your Second Leg

In the world of building communities, there are many strategies and approaches. However, in our experience, we have found that some practices work better than others. When we find one that works, we teach it uniformly across the board and duplicate that proven technique throughout the organization. One such area that we have analyzed for years is the appropriate time to begin one's second leg. Of course, it's your business, and you can do whatever you wish. However, we can make some strong recommendations aligned with what we've seen work and not work in the past. One such area of prime importance is the beginning of the second leg.

Proficiency is the key consideration. Before you place someone at the top of a new leg (in essence, "starting your second leg"), it is very advisable to gain some experience in community building first. As mentioned above, we call this the apprenticeship process. This is where you work with your upline (the team of people you joined) to place people you find into your first leg and, in turn, help those people get started properly. This gives you experience, gets you acquainted with the process, and enables you to know what to do with the people you'll be starting atop your second leg.

Therefore, it is recommended that you wait to begin your second leg until after you have:

1. Become a Professional Business Owner (PBO) yourself
2. Contributed at least two people from your own names list to your first leg
— 3. Helped those two people you brought into the business (or at least two people *they* brought into the business) become PBOs themselves
4. Attained a total of four PBOs in that first leg
5. Attained at least ten people deep overall in that first leg

Once you have completed this list, you will be ready to begin your second leg with the next LIFE Member you bring into the business. Also, fulfilling this list of recommendations sets up the first part of the qualification for Power Player.

Note that in building one leg to this level first before beginning another, you are satisfying Robert Kiyosaki's *Three Keys to Wealth* mentioned in chapter two. Practically, this ensures that you have served an amount of time as an apprentice and learned by both watching and participating. By the time you turn loose on your second leg, you will have some basic experience and results under your belt. This will not only make you more effective, but it will also give you some credibility.

Orchestrate

The fastest teams orchestrate depth in an organization. Each LIFE Member commits to contributing to the growth at the bottom, and a team of such leaders forms to hold each other accountable. If you are new to building communities, orchestration will only work *after* you have proven yourself to be a strong learner of community building *and* you have had success as a top performer in your team. To orchestrate before this will just be

126

viewed as management to those you are trying to lead. And trying to manage a volunteer-type organization is like pouring oil into water; it won't mix. But if you are performing, people will naturally want to follow you. The types of activities you can coordinate involve large group meetings, where you can plug multiple people, organizations, and even legs together to maximize your time. Also, you can orchestrate squeeze board meetings as described above.

Orchestration results from thinking through your business and attempting to accomplish everything you can with as many people as you can in everything you do. As your business grows bigger and bigger, there will be more and more opportunities for this, and in turn, thoughtful orchestration will help you grow faster and faster.

Master the Pattern

To become good at building depth in an organization, one must master the Five-Step Pattern of making a list, contacting the people on that list, showing them the plan, following through, and getting them started properly. The way to master something is to study the theory and repeatedly apply the theory to actual practice. Listen to the audios relating to the pattern, read through the literature, and show the plan as much and as often as you can. Also, review this textbook regularly. (We certainly didn't write this for the fun of it!) Do this over and over. Proficiency comes through repetition. It may also help you to memorize key phrases that you find useful in each of the five steps. Consult your upline or mentor to analyze your performance and make adjustments.

There is nothing complicated about rotating the pattern. In fact, anyone with basic faculties can do it. Making a list just involves writing down some names. Contacting people simply means calling them. Showing the plan is just having a conversation. Following through is having an additional conversation. And rotating the pattern on their behalf is simply repeating what you've just done. Everybody can do these steps, but those who choose to do them repeatedly and to the point of getting good at them will have the biggest and fastest growing businesses. This also means that they will make the most money!

Being Bad to Get Good

To become good at something, you normally have to start out by first being bad at it. That's okay. All things worth doing well are worth doing badly until you can learn to do them well. And the only reason you may not be great at these steps at first is because they are new to you. Chances are you weren't a star performer your first day at your job either. A certain amount of time was required to get acquainted with the surroundings, learn what was expected, and gain proficiency. Community building is no different. Give yourself time to get good at it because LIFE Leadership can work so well that it just might be the last thing you'll ever have to get good at (financially speaking)!

Focus

Focus is also required to build depth. When drawing out diagrams of depth in an organization, everything looks neat and tidy. But it won't feel that way as you learn to drive depth. That is because you are not constructing an organization of *diagrams*; you are constructing an organization of *people*. And that's where everything gets interesting. People are wonderful and frustrating all at the same time. They are predictable and unpredictable. They are hot and cold, rude and polite, mature and immature, ambitious (we like the word *hungry* better) and lazy. And all those conflicts can exist within just one person!

It is up to you to stay focused on the objective of building a deep organization, even with an apparent complexity of multiple people with differing personalities and levels of interest becoming involved in your business. In one way, you have to make a connection with people and love them for being the special individuals they are. In another way, you must stay focused on moving the bottom of your team deeper, no matter what.

Developing People Skills

We cannot, in any way, overemphasize this point: The ability to deal successfully with people will be absolutely required in order to build depth. As Robert Kiyosaki wrote, **"Your success or failure as an entrepreneur depends a lot on your people skills.** If you have strong people skills, your business will grow. If you have poor people skills, your business will suffer." We believe this to be truer in this industry. That is the reason there is a strong emphasis on developing people skills and personal growth in the LIFE Training Marketing System. Four of our "Top 5 Books" are aimed directly at helping readers develop better people skills. These four books are *How to Win Friends and Influence People* by Dale Carnegie, *How I Raised Myself from Failure to Success in Selling* by Frank Bettger, *How to Have Confidence and Power in Dealing with People* by Les Giblin, and *Personality Plus* by Florence Littauer.

Whenever you hear a LIFE Member talking about his team, saying, "I can't get these people to..." or "The people on my team won't..." or "Why won't they...?" it is a good indication that there may be a lack of people skills on the part of that LIFE Member. Our experience is that people generally have a higher opinion of themselves in the area of people skills than the facts actually allow. As one saying goes, "Reality and self-assessment are often very far apart."

The ability to deal with people is key. Even the very best among us should continue to study and improve. When it comes to effectively dealing with others, we never "arrive." We are always on the journey. With the LIFE Training system, we know that journey will be in the positive direction. Sadly, with what the world generally feeds people, the journey is actually backwards. This is yet another reason why the LIFE Training tools are so critical. We must unlearn the bad habits with which we came into the industry and overcome the daily challenges that face us all at the same time.

Do we really listen to people? Are we really good at making friends? Are we able to overcome shyness and self-consciousness and reach out to others? Can we remember names and important details about people? Do we truly care about others? Are we unselfish and interested in serving other people? These questions and others ought to be our constant test to see how we are doing in the area of developing people skills. Growing personally in this area will be required to grow a big business, but it will also bring rewards in every area of your life. Get committed to improving your people skills, no matter how good they may already be. Depth in your organization depends on it!

Don't Hand Off Responsibility

To build depth in an organization, you will have to do it yourself. Team Approach is one thing, but ultimately, as we discussed before, "If it's to be, it's up to me." That is the only attitude that will result in a business that continually grows deeper and deeper. For depth to happen, you must take full responsibility yourself for making it grow.

Too many times, we've seen people get involved in building depth in their organization and make one of two key mistakes. First, they expect their upline leader to build it for them. "When are you going to do more to help me?" and "When are you going to drive depth under me?" and "How deep did you make it grow this week?" are all questions asked by people suffering from this mistake. The other mistake is to think that someone below you in your organization will take over the building of depth for you. We call this "handing off of leadership responsibility." "Oh, I've got Bob and Mary in that group. They're going to go all the way. So I'll just counsel them and encourage them" is the kind of thing said or thought by those suffering from this mistake.

Here is the best way to avoid either of these errors: Never assume anyone else will ever do anything. **Take responsibility for doing it yourself.** If someone else contributes, great! All the better. If not, no big deal; you were going to do it anyway. Besides, the people in your organization will copy the example they see from you. If you expect your upline to build your business for you, others will expect the same coddling from you. If you hand off responsibility to someone in your group, they will do the same thing to people in their group. Leadership is not "handed" to anyone; it must be taken. When you are building your business properly, driving depth and building teams, people who crave leadership and responsibility will spring up in your organizations. They will begin doing the right things, copying what they see their upline doing, and moving the business forward on their own efforts. They will take responsibility for their actions and results. It is when you start to have people like this in your organization that a transfer and sharing of leadership takes place. But it can never be "handed" or assigned to someone; it must be taken in this way—by force!

By avoiding either of these mistakes, you set a very visible example in your organization that others will copy. This will lead to faster growth, more harmonious teams, and more income!

There is another warning we should give here. One of the most common mistakes is for people to get into something we call "management mode." This is a condition where they begin telling others how to do the business and trying to teach others all that they know instead of simply building it themselves. Often, the people doing this fake themselves out by thinking that this is *leadership or mentoring.* (For an in-depth explanation of the difference between management and leadership, see our book *Launching a Leadership Revolution.*) Management mode is as far from leadership or mentoring as one can get! We can never mentor someone when we are new. Also, **we can never mentor someone when we don't have significant success and experience ourselves.** And we can never mentor someone else if we are not being mentored in turn. Finally, we can never mentor or teach someone to do something that we aren't doing ourselves! Until you have significant (and we mean *significant*) success and experience in the business, your responsibility for the grooming and leading of your people is the following:

1. Love your people.
2. Work more than they do.
3. Point to the LIFE Training Marketing System, *not* to your own teaching!
4. Drive depth underneath them.

Being Creative but Not Inventive

Over time, you will develop your own style within the framework of the pattern. There will always be room for you to be yourself and express your own personal style, to a degree, of course. But don't forget that the pattern is *proven*. Become inventive at your own peril. Following the pattern as it is and mastering each step will allow you to show the plan, get to the next person, show the plan a level deeper, and develop massive depth in your organization. Changing things, even a little, can take you off course. When you are just starting out or when your group is small, this might not seem like such a big deal. But over time, being a little off course can take you way off.

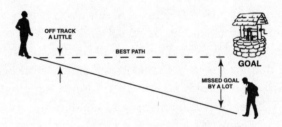

Also, as we explained above, being too inventive gets copied by your organization and can quickly lead to a mess. You'll have people everywhere thinking their little tweaks are the greatest inventions in the world. At best, nothing will get accomplished because chaos cannot build a community, only a mob. And at worst, your business will resemble a mob and become unruly and destructive. We don't mean this literally, of course. But figuratively, we've seen it happen. So stay within the proven techniques of the pattern. Get as creative as you want in terms of creating a team, creating depth, creating new relationships, and creating massive product flow. But avoid getting inventive.

Would the boy you were be proud of the man you are?
—Anonymous

We make a living by what we get. But we make a life by what we give.
—Unknown (sometimes attributed to Winston Churchill)

Mastery is not something that strikes in an instant, like a thunderbolt, but a gathering power that moves steadily through time, like weather.
—John Champlin Gardner

People forget how fast you did a job, but they remember how well you did it.
—Howard N. Newton

I would rather take a thousand "No"s than one "I told you so"!
—Orrin Woodward

Name: DETAIL DAN
Quote: "I just have a few more questions. Suppose I sponsored my cousin in the Virgin Islands, and then he moved to Malta and married an Italian. Would his bonus checks convert to lira, euros, or dollars?"

CHAPTER 9

RESULTS, PART TWO
CONQUER, FORTIFY, DOMESTICATE

Being in business is not about being in "busyness." It is about getting things done—for the sake of having a better life! For a LIFE Member, being busy doesn't make you successful; it only makes you tired! This is where becoming an entrepreneur can differ from a life in the corporate world. Many times as an employee, what is rewarded is seniority, attitude, one's relationship with the boss, the number of hours worked regardless of their effectiveness, and other factors that may or may not have anything to do with what an individual is actually accomplishing.

For entrepreneurs, it is different. Looking the part, playing the games, and "talking the talk" will get you nowhere in the real world of owning your own business. To *make it,* you have to *make it happen.* You have to hold yourself accountable for results.

The best way to keep yourself on track, honest about your performance, and improving all the time is by properly measuring your performance. No sport would be interesting to watch or play if the participants didn't have a scoreboard to know how they are doing. As a matter of fact, some have theorized that sports are such a popular entertainment for so many people exactly *because* immediate feedback is provided regarding how a team or individual is performing. Such is the life of an entrepreneur, also.

The way to understand your business properly is to know that you must learn to *lead people* and *manage the numbers.* This is like breathing. You don't only breathe in, and you don't only breathe out. You must do *both.* In business, you must learn to become adept at both managing the numbers *and* leading the people. This chapter will focus on managing the numbers.

Conquer, Fortify, Domesticate

Throughout history there have been battles all over the face of the globe. In times past (and sometimes still today), much of the conflict was over territory. One ruler wanted the land that another ruler possessed. Ultimately, this conflict would lead to war, and armies would take to the field. In such a situation, the first aim of an army was to *conquer* new territory by taking it from the opposing army.

Next, once an area had been overtaken and the enemy had been driven off, the victorious army would *fortify* that area, or secure its position. It would accomplish this by digging into the earth to erect breastworks and redoubts and by building barricades or forts to keep the enemy from retaking the territory.

After a while, once the "coast was clear" and the enemy was safely repulsed from the territory, the area could then be *domesticated*. Settlers would be brought in to till the soil, women and children would come to live with their conquering heroes, and new towns and villages would be built.

Thankfully, LIFE Leadership does not require us to raise arms against an enemy. But it is a lot like a battle in that we have to *conquer* new territory in terms of growing our business bigger, *fortify* it by making it secure and long-lasting, and *domesticate* it by moving life-changing information through it. These three steps are a good reminder of the order of attack when building our organizations as well as the proper measurements to consider when checking our progress and assessing the strength of our teams.

It is always a temptation to focus on too many things. People can run off in all directions doing this or that. But as we have said before, the most successful LIFE Members always subscribe to the "What's Important Next?" theory of doing things. They know that there are always many *good* things to do but only one or two *great* things. Focusing on doing the great things at the expense of the good things is called prioritization. It is the proper prioritization of your business that the illustration of *conquer, fortify, domesticate* is designed to teach.

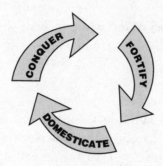

Incidentally, we could also relabel this diagram as Product, Process, and Program.

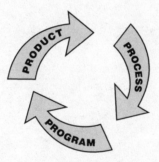

Further, as we have been discussing, we could also refer to this concept as Information, Progress, and Income.

These labels are simply meant to provide helpful markers on the concepts that are central to building a community of people through which products flow. For the purpose of this chapter, we will continue to refer to these concepts using the Conquer, Fortify, and Domesticate labels. (You will also hear this same terminology used on many LIFE Training audios).

Conquer

The first priority in building a community is one of conquering new territory. This involves introducing your business to new people. There are very few things that could be considered more important or more productive in the building of your business.

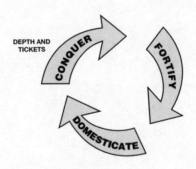

Odometer and Speedometer

When it comes to measuring your business, there are really two categories that you should be tracking. One can be called an odometer measurement. An odometer on a car tells you how many total miles the vehicle has traveled. An odometer measurement of your business tells you how big it is. It basically measures the size of your team. However, an odometer gives no indication as to the speed of the growth of your business, so another gauge is required, that of the speedometer. A speedometer on a car, obviously, tells you how fast the vehicle is traveling. Likewise, in your business, you will be very interested to know and measure the speed of growth of your team. **When it comes to the principles of monitoring your business, these are the two main categories at**

which you will be looking: the size of your business and the speed of your business's growth.

Depth

The natural state of the business is growth, just like a healthy child. "Holding your own" or "treading water" is not healthy for a business. A key measurement you should be using to track the health and progress of your business is the magnitude and the pace at which the depth is happening in each of your organizations. When we talk about speedometer readings, this is a prime example. How many levels deeper is your business growing every week at the bottom of each leg?

Depth is a great concept, and it is our major strategic weapon. But it must be employed properly, and that means quickly. There is a pace to success, and it must be high enough to generate excitement and belief up through the organization. If depth grows too slowly, people can start to doubt the business and, worse, their own ability to build it. But if depth grows quickly, people will get energized, confident, and active.

So keep track of the levels of depth you develop on a weekly basis. Counsel with your upline to determine the appropriate levels of depth for which you should be aiming. Then make sure you are on pace. Make sure you are aiming at Power Player and accomplishing it in a fast enough amount of time. Remember, momentum is your best friend in this industry. Go after it!

The *number of levels* in depth of your business is an *odometer* reading. It tells how big your business is. The *pace* at which your depth is progressing is a *speedometer* reading. It tells how fast your business is growing. Monitor both of these aspects of depth to get a clear picture.

Number of Total Access Subscriptions

Another important measure for your business in the Conquer category is the number of people attending the Monthly Seminars (or watching them on webcasts) being held around the world. This is your real "team" or "community": the people who are attending the events and associating with other successful people in the business. It is at the events where they will receive the information, the inspiration, and the belief needed to move on. The best way to track this is through the number of people subscribing to the Total Access product. These are those who are on subscription for access to all of the Open Meeting and Monthly Seminar events (in other words, those who have taken Step 2 of the Next Step Program). This is one of the most important measurements to track as you conquer new territory and one of the key areas in which you should set monthly goals.

Fortify

The next most important thing to do, after conquering new territory, is to fortify the new territory you have gained. This means strengthening your new community to make it more secure. This is accomplished by involving your organization in the LIFE Training Marketing System. It will also start the people in your group on a path toward personal growth and learning that is the prerequisite to success in the Information Age. Additionally, it will help "beat back" the daily doses of negativity that people receive out there in the world. We call this the Media War—fighting negative, dream-robbing, complacency-building media with positive, champion-enabling media.

So the Fortify step is really a measure of how well you have *systematized* your team. The best way to do this, of course, is to make sure you have systematized yourself first. Become a "tool" expert. Become a tool dispenser. Make the training system work for you by having items on hand and leveraging them liberally. Spreading tools around society is a lot like planting seeds for a future harvest. Want a bigger business? Plant more tools! Understanding this, the new diagram would look like this:

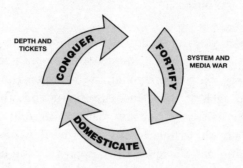

LIFE Training Marketing System Subscriptions

If fortifying your business is important, as we said before, then the number of business owners in your team who are on the LIFE Training system is a good measurement of results (these are those LIFE Members who have taken Step 3 of the Next Step Program and are subscribing to the LIFE Training Marketing System). The information in the Marketing System goes out to the entire organization all at the same time, all over the world, and gives everybody the same information. In this Information Age in which we live, having access to the correct information on a timely basis has never been so critical. Having that information pure, timely, and, most important, in a duplicatable fashion is fertilizer to the growth of your business. In LIFE Leadership, we have never seen anyone achieve any significant level of product flow, organization size, or growth without the use of the Marketing System. While it is optional, it has proven to be one of the best measurements of how well an organization is being trained, is maintaining its attitude, and is moving forward.

Marketing System subscriptions are primarily an odometer reading that tells you the size of your organization, but by making comparisons to previous weeks, you can get a feel for the speedometer side of the business, too. You should aim for an increase in your LIFE Training Marketing System count every week.

Special Order Tools

We have been talking about different ways to measure and monitor your business in order to track your performance and stay on target toward your goals and dreams. However, there is one aspect to each of these measurements that they all have in common: they can only indicate what is actually happening in your business at that time. In other words, they have only limited *predictive* value as to what will happen in your business in the future.

To explain, let's consider the trading of stocks, for instance, in which there are two schools of thought as to the best way to go about it. The first method, called *fundamental* stock trading, focuses on exactly that: the fundamentals of a particular business. How is that business performing? How talented is the management team? What do their financials look like? And other questions like these are considered. A second method, called *technical* trading, focuses on something entirely different. For every company with a publicly traded stock, there is a chart that shows the history of activity regarding that stock. Actually, there are many charts. These charts show the fluctuation of price over time. They also show price versus the volume of shares traded, the size of blocks traded at a time, etc. According to technical traders, it is possible to determine the quality of an investment merely by reading the charts properly. A valuable piece of information to have would be the predictive value of whether or not the price of a stock were about to go up or down. A feature on a chart that gives such a prediction is called a *leading indicator*. It indicates what will happen *before* it actually happens.

In similar fashion, special order tools are the best leading indicator in our business. Special order tools are training aids and support materials that are ordered above and beyond anything that is received with the LIFE Training Marketing System subscription. Almost without exception, whenever an organization has a high hunger level for special order tools, the group is about to encounter explosive growth. This is due to several reasons.

First of all, tools are key in expanding a business because they are the purest form of teaching available. With an audio recording, the speaker giving a talk about a certain topic delivers it the exact same way every time! Everybody and anybody who listens to it anywhere in the world gets to hear the exact same talk. This is the purest form of duplication available because everybody gets the same message. People can also listen to the talk repeatedly, heightening their understanding and education.

Second, when tools are moving through an organization, it is proof that the leader or leaders in that group are committed to growing their business. Nobody invests in tools to hand out to people unless he or she is planning on showing the plan to some people and handing them the tools! For that reason, when tools are flowing, you can rest assured that there are about to be a lot of plans shown in that group. And remember, your business grows based on the number of exposures to new people.

Third, tools broaden the relatability of the person showing the plan. Let's face it; we each have a special personality all our own. That fact can be both good and bad! Try as we might, with all the people skills we can learn, we are just not going to relate to everybody. That's where the tools come in. Even if a particular prospect did not relate very well to you during the plan, chances are high that he or she will relate to somebody else on the audios. In this way, the tools broaden your relatability and increase your chances of connecting the right people to your business.

Finally, tools are so important to your business because they carry the truth. The books, CDs, DVDs, downloads, pamphlets, etc. focus on helping people unlearn the wrong teachings they may have absorbed all their lives and finally learn the right stuff. It is common for us to hear new people say things like, "Where has this information been all my life?" and "Why didn't they teach me this stuff in school?" and "If I had only known about you guys sooner!" As the saying goes, "Truth is sweet to the ears." People know the truth when they hear it, especially those who have been hungering for it.

For these reasons, make sure you have an appropriate stock of extra tools (and also LIFE Leadership products, of course) to provide to people. And everywhere you go, **promote tools like seeds of a future harvest**. You can't reap if you don't sow.

The Media War

The Information Age has changed all the rules. Those with the correct information win. Those with wrong information lose. How old you are, how much experience you have, or how long you have been with your employer doesn't matter. When the rules change, they change for *everybody*. Adapt to the new rules, or get left behind.

The new rules say that information is king. Success will depend on getting the correct information and acting on it. That is exactly what the LIFE Training system of materials and meetings is designed to do. How do we know our system contains the "right" information? Because the information we have applied has worked. We know we are nothing special. We had tried our hardest acting on Industrial-Age advice in an Industrial-Age system with Industrial-Age companies. What we got were mediocre results. We had an inferior set of operating principles, or inferior *information*. Then, someone connected us to mentors who actually had succeeded financially and understood the rules of the new economy. We simply started listening and then applied our efforts in that direction. It worked. We are the same guys, but we experienced vastly different results. *That's* the value of the information. *That's* the value of learning the truth about business, finance, people, personal growth, entrepreneurship, and the Information Age. And *that's* what the LIFE Training Marketing System does.

Each one of us every day receives hundreds of messages from the world about how to live, what to wear, how to act, what to buy, and what our values should be. We are bombarded by television, newspaper, radio, music, e-mail, junk mail, junk e-mail, pop-ups, spam, news, magazines, and association with people we may or may not choose to spend so much time with (fellow employees, for example). This is junk food for junk thinking. Learning proper thinking, learning *wealth thinking*, will involve the undoing and the "beating back" of some of these destructive inputs. That's what the LIFE Training system does. And as you can see, it becomes a war of information. It becomes a *Media War*.

We have chosen to delve into this concept here because how well you do in waging the Media War will really be the indicator of how well you are building your business. The LIFE Training system doesn't compete with other word-of-mouth marketing companies. It doesn't compete with other sales endeavors. It doesn't compete with other businesses, at all. What it competes with is the message of mediocrity that the world continues to sell us: a message that says we *can't* make it big, we *don't* deserve success, that playing small is somehow noble, that success is for "somebody else," and that doing "pretty good" is good enough. As author Bill Perkins wrote, "No weapon...has been more effective than the barrage of propaganda that hammers away at our thinking and convinces us we're not warriors. It urges us to kick back and watch the world pass by like a parade. Such passivity reeks of danger."

LIFE Leadership stands directly opposed to such passivity. We know that every person has the seeds of greatness inside, and we use our tools and our training system to water and nurture those seeds. We have seen people the world had left behind get involved in our training system and thrive through the information received. We have witnessed others who were hooked on status and *looking good* actually learn to *truly* do well in life. We have watched as people struggling in the grip of addictions broke free and began to regain control and dignity because of the inspiration they received from our training system. Now don't get us wrong; we are not taking credit for this. We don't have all the answers. But we know the power of the truth. We have seen it firsthand, in our own lives and in the lives of others, and we are committed to spreading it as far as we possibly can.

Do you really want to know how well your business is doing? Do you want an accurate unit of measure? Take a look at how well the people who have chosen to join with you are doing. Have you done all that you can to get the truth into their hands? Have you seen them change because of something they heard on an audio or read in a book? Have you had people open up with you and share challenges because they want to grow and improve? Have you seen negative attitudes turn into positive ones? Have you seen husbands start treating their wives better? Have you seen wives treating their husbands better? Have you seen people's hearts grow warmer and warmer? As you build your business, look for those types of things in the lives of the people who enter your organization. *That's* the heart of success in this industry. Actually, that's the heart of success in *life* (no pun intended)! **Make your ultimate measure of success in your business journey the number of people you help along the way. Oh yeah, and as a result, you'll probably make some money, too.**

Domesticate

Domesticating your business means making sure that you develop product flow through the organization you have created. This is the step where you help people learn how to move LIFE Leadership materials.

There are several ways in which LIFE Leadership products flow. One is to sell to customers. Another is for Members to subscribe to the materials themselves. In short, products flow three ways:

1. Products handed out as advertisement
2. Purchases made by customers
3. Personal use by LIFE Members

It is important to note again at this point that your organization will duplicate the example they see in you. If you expect products to move through your organization, and if you expect to be effective at retailing them to customers, be sure to move them and utilize them yourself! There is no story like the story you can tell from personal experience.

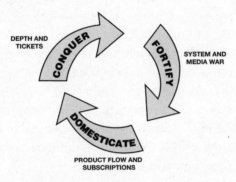

Subscription Programs

When discussing results in your business and how to track them properly, we must ultimately get down to talking about *product flow*. After all, you build communities for the purpose of moving products and receiving the profits from those sales. And by far, the best way we have ever encountered for moving products through a community is through a subscription program, to both customers and LIFE Members.

Subscriptions are nice because they generate an ongoing flow of products to your customers. This is important for three reasons. The first is because it has been our experience that the best, most impactful programs for changing lives occur in little doses taken consistently over time. This is the most relevant way to go about creating new habits in someone's life. And it's the formation of those new habits that produces lasting change. Second, this makes any program more affordable because it is split into little bite-size pieces, and the cost is spread out over time. Third, this leads to an ongoing residual income for the LIFE Member who has customers subscribing to products. Each month as the customer receives his or her shipment of life-changing products, the LIFE Member receives his or her 25 percent commission, plus bonuses. So, while it is nice to sell individual products, and that will always be a big part of your business, it is extremely effective to enlist your customers on product subscriptions for all these reasons.

Tracking the number of LIFE Members on subscription lets you know how well the basic building block of moving products is duplicating in your group. If you have new sign-ups, but they aren't getting involved with the subscriptions (meaning, they aren't subscribing to one, two, or more of the subscription series available from LIFE Leadership, and they aren't attracting retail customers who are subscribing), somebody needs to be educated on the principles of duplication and "what's in it for them." Remember, it's the principle of *duplication* that leads to massive businesses. Discretion and divergence don't. Monitor your subscription numbers (on the lifeleadership.com website) to check your team's strength in this area.

Perhaps at this point, it may be helpful to relate a little story about one of the world's most successful professional athletes because most people don't understand what it means to be "under contract" to represent a certain product. They join a business and don't necessarily understand that, just like a high-profile professional athlete, they too now have a contract with a manufacturer that pays them for loyalty and increased product usage. The athlete to which we refer is Michael Jordan. In the book *Driven from Within,* Jordan's best friend relates a story that illustrates the loyalty and commitment that not only propelled Jordan to the top of the sporting world but to the top of the product endorsement world as well.

According to Fred Whitfield:

> Michael's whole being is about loyalty and winning. He really feels like you can't ride the fence. You have got to be loyal to what you believe in, and then always believe you're

going to win. That's probably what I have learned from him over all these years.

I was really close to Ralph Sampson. Ralph had a big Puma contract coming out of the University of Virginia. He was Puma's man. When I would go up to Boston with Ralph, we'd go to the Puma warehouse. I would do the same thing when I'd go out to Nike with Michael. They'd say, "Whatever you want, pick it out and we'll ship it to you." I had my closet separated out, half Puma, half Nike. I had 25 or 30 pairs of Pumas....Then I had all my Air Jordans, Nike stuff.

Michael comes to my apartment in Greensboro one time. We're getting ready to go out, and he says, "Man, it's kind of cold. Can I borrow one of your jackets?" I said, sure, go in my closet. He went in there and saw everything separated out. He's in there a little longer than necessary, and here he comes out of my room.

He's taken all my Puma stuff, brought it out into the living room and laid it on the floor. He goes into the kitchen, gets a butcher knife and literally cuts up everything. This was like his second or third year in the league. He literally took a butcher knife, and he's inside the suede shoes, ripping, cutting. When he's all done, he picks up every little scrap and walks it all down to the dumpster.

He says, "Hey dude, call Howard tomorrow and tell him to replace all of this. But don't ever let me see you in anything other than Nike. You can't ride the fence." From that day forward, I've never worn anything that wasn't Nike. That's the degree to which he believes.

If you walk into a room with Michael, the first thing he's going to do is look at you from head to toe. He's going to look at your feet.

We share this story in its entirety not because it shows how extreme Michael Jordan is but because it shows how well he understands business. When it comes to loyalty, *99 percent loyalty is 100 percent disloyalty*. Jordan understood that he was being paid to do a job. And he became the biggest "business" professional athlete the sporting world had yet seen and set the standard for all athletes to follow.

Jordan understood that the master copy had to be worth copying. In our industry, which runs on the concept of duplication, it should be equally important for us to be product loyal. Now don't get us wrong; we are certainly not promoting the idea that you should show up with tin snips and start cutting up your business partner's shoes! But the principle of loyalty should be clear. Set a strong example yourself, and measure the number of people loyal to their own products and setting customers up on the product subscriptions to track your business's health. Teach everyone to develop at least some of Michael Jordan's professional attitude!

Trip Tracking

There's another advantage to having the kind of loyalty Michael Jordan demonstrated for his friend that day. Remember when we were talking about the exciting incentive trips and paid vacations? Well, part of the qualification for receiving those wonderful trips is to maintain a minimum of at least 200 PV per month running through your business. This means customer volume, personal use, and samples handed out. As long as the total is 200 PV or more each month (running through your personal LIFE Leadership number), you have met what is called the "Trip Tracking" requirement. Trip Tracking begins whenever you start generating 200 PV or more each month in your business (while meeting all customer requirements) and do that consistently month after month (see the "LIFE Leadership Compensation Plan and Income Disclosure Statement" brochure for detailed information regarding the incentive trips). So loyalty like Jordan's is part of what gets you qualified for those wonderful trips.

Power Player Measurements

Now that we understand the theory and specifics of building depth, it is time to go back to the Power Player Program. And remember, accomplishing or "going" Power Player tells you if you are building the business properly. You may recall that the Power Player Program encompasses three main components of building your business: *theory*, *activity*, and *results*. We went through those earlier at a high level. Now let's dig into the details of specifically what needs to be accomplished for a LIFE Member to be called a Power Player.

To accomplish Power Player and receive the recognition and prestige that go along with it (not to mention the business growth that results from its accomplishment), a business owner must build his or her personal organization (first leg) ten levels deep and a second personal organization (second leg) five levels deep. Additionally, the leg that is ten levels deep must have a minimum of four Professional Business Owners (PBOs) in it. And the second leg must have a minimum of two Professional Business Owners (PBOs). See the diagram below.

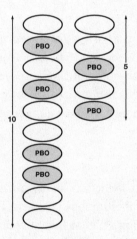

You can easily track new growth by using your LIFE Leadership Calendar or LIFE Leadership Member Tracking Board (both available on the Shopping Center at lifeladership.com) to keep it straight.

The other part of the Power Player requirement is moving 200 points through your personal business, not including the volume generated by other Members on your team. This volume can include products you have purchased to use yourself as well as those you have retailed to customers and used as advertisement.

When the theory and activity requirements of Power Player have consistently been filled and the results have been accomplished, the LIFE Member is immediately recognized as a Power Player! Below is a summary of what is required in each of the categories of Theory, Activity, and Results in order to be called a Power Player:

Theory

1. Be a Professional Business Owner (PBO) yourself.
2. Purchase and listen to the *Top 50 CD Pack*.
3. Attend Open Meetings and Night Owls.
4. Attend Monthly Seminars.
5. Attend Leadership Conventions.

Activity

1. Show at least an average of fifteen plans each month. The plans can be shown to people from your list and/or to people from the lists of those in depth.
2. Generate 200 PV per month (all of which can be customer volume). And meet all customer requirements.

Results

1. Build one leg at least ten levels in depth with at least four Professional Business Owners (PBOs) in it.
2. Build a second leg at least five new levels in depth with at least two Professional Business Owners (PBOs) in it.

Once you have accomplished Power Player, however, it is *not* time to take a rest. The worst thing in the world you can do after a major accomplishment is to take a rest. Why? Because that kills all the momentum you've developed. Feel free to celebrate for a moment; after all, you've earned it. But quickly get back to work on the path toward your dreams. The proper thing to do is to keep the momentum going and qualify for Power Player again, which effectively would be what we call a Double Power Player. Now to do that, it doesn't mean you have to do twice the amount of monthly theory or activity, but it does mean that you have to achieve twice the amount of *results*. So a Double Power Player would be a business owner who achieved the monthly theory and activity requirements while building a leg twenty deep with a minimum of eight PBOs and a second leg ten deep with a minimum of four PBOs. The monthly product volume requirement would stay the same.

Feel free also to continue the momentum even further from Double Power Player to Triple, Quad, Penta, Hexa, and beyond! The Members who have accomplished these levels obviously have had the fastest growing businesses.

Summary

Knowing what to measure in the performance of your business will go a long way toward staying on track and producing consistent, sustaining growth. Remember, the principle is to lead people and manage numbers.

You can't build a reputation on what you are going to do.
—Henry Ford

You can spend your whole life any way you want to, but you can only spend it once.
—Dwight Thompson

Life is not a dress rehearsal.
—Peter Daniels

As long as you're green, you're growing. As soon as you're ripe, you start to rot.
—Ray Kroc

There is no more miserable human being than the one in whom nothing is habitual but indecision.
—William James

Name: FRAIDY-CAT FRED
Quote: "Oh, um, my list? I just can't
         seem to find it. It's not really
         done anyway. Besides, I really
         need to study that contacting
         script for a few more weeks
         before I make any calls."

CHAPTER 10

BUSINESS OWNERSHIP
THE PRINCIPLES

Now that we have surveyed the wealth of information available on how to build a community of people through which life-changing information flows, it is time to put it all together. There are many overarching principles and a host of specifics that are required to complete the package. In this chapter, we will focus on the principles, which will make all the steps we've discussed so far not only easier to accomplish but also more fruitful.

Deny Yourself

One of the most important things to learn about becoming a business owner, whether in LIFE Leadership or any other profession, is to deny yourself. We live in an instant gratification world. Everybody wants things right now, and they want them to be perfect and easy. Unfortunately, none of that is reality, especially when talking about greatness and success. These things take time, and they take the application of self-discipline. As mathematician and philosopher Pythagoras said centuries ago, "Make self-control a habit."

It is okay to keep good things from yourself so that you can later earn great things. It is okay to do without for a little while. It is okay to go backward to go forward. And it is okay to be tough on yourself and allow yourself to struggle. You will never see a champion who babies him- or herself or has to give in to every whim and urge. Self-discipline, and the ability to give up in the short term so that you can obtain in the long term, is not only a sign of maturity, but it is also a prerequisite to success and significance. And it is a choice. As a business owner, be sure to make that choice daily.

Be Consistent

As we discussed earlier in this book, little things lead to big things. But this is only true if those little things are done properly and *consistently*. As author Alexander Lockhart wrote, "The success or failure of your life depends not so much on how hard you try, but the accumulation of your efforts, and whether you keep at it." For efforts to accumulate, they must be consistent.

In LIFE Leadership, it is common for people to get really excited and begin taking the correct steps. Then suddenly, something pops up to distract them. Maybe a promotion comes up at work, a family struggle occurs, a new romance blooms, football season starts, the kids go back to school, or it's time to clip their finger nails. We've seen it time and time again; people get off to a great start, they begin developing momentum in their learning and in their business, and then they let the smallest thing knock them off course. One of our favorite quotes is, "Most men fail because of broken focus." Focus is the secret weapon of a champion. Talent and effort can only bear fruit as a result of focus, and consistent focus at that. There is a legend that the wise philosopher Aristotle was once asked by a passerby, "How do you get to Mount Olympus?" to which the great sage replied, "By ensuring that each step you take is in that direction." That's the meaning of consistency: ensure that each step is in the right direction.

How does one stay consistent in this profession? After all, knowing that one should stay consistent and actually *remaining* consistent are two different things. The answer lies in the power of your dreams to motivate you. The best way to stay consistent is to stay committed to your dreams. Look at your dreams regularly. The basic concept is that you won't be properly driven to achieve greater results in your life until you familiarize yourself with what those results could be. This might involve going to look at new homes, test driving a new car, or simply visualizing your last day at work. If we deny the power of our dreams, we deny one of the biggest sources of power within us, a power that can drive us to be consistent. Another way to stay consistent is to stay plugged into the LIFE Training Marketing System. Listening to audios, watching videos, reading the books, and associating with other LIFE Members who are excited about achieving their dreams cannot help but build consistency. Just realize this: Consistency is one of your best friends. Treat him properly, and he will reward you accordingly.

Set the Example

Albert Schweitzer once said, "Example isn't the main thing in influencing other people. It is the only thing." While there are some who wouldn't take it quite that far, there can be no debating the importance of personal example in any enterprise. This is doubly true in LIFE Leadership, which is all about relationships with other people. Those people will look to you for a map on how to behave, conduct their own business, and respond to situations.

This surprises most people when they are new to this industry. Perhaps they have lived their lives, earned their money, and spent their time in ways where they didn't have to face up to how their behavior affected other human beings. But all of us have an effect on others. And to build a strong business, you must be conscious of your example and make sure it is a good one, even if it is the first time you've ever had to do so. This is because LIFE Leadership builds on a concept called *duplication*, which we've already covered and will still discuss in greater detail in a little while. For now, suffice it to say that duplication is the idea that the master will be copied, in all ways, good and bad. If you have a bad attitude, that attitude will duplicate down through your organization (and likewise with a good attitude). If you are short with people, selfish, lazy, or possess any other negative attitude, you will surely see signs of those attitudes showing up in your group. But if you are patient, selfless, energetic, and positive, you should see a group of people copying your example. Of course, we don't live in a perfect world. And the following humorous saying rings only too true: "Your group will duplicate 100 percent of the things you do wrong and only about 50 percent of the things you do right." For this reason, we'd better be extra careful with our personal example and make sure it is a good one!

Expect the Best out of People

Any fool can find fault; it takes somebody special to find greatness. In order to build a big business, it becomes absolutely necessary that we see the good in other people. Some have called this "becoming a good-finder." Others have suggested the best way to do this is to "catch others in the act of doing something right." Whatever the recipe, it is important to understand the power you have in the lives of others when you hold them to a standard and expect them to live up to it.

This doesn't mean that you impose your iron will on people. And it doesn't mean that they have to perform to satisfy your demands. What it involves is meeting people where they are but expecting them to become the best they can be. It is the difference between mere friendship and something that heads in the direction of mentorship. A friend will allow you to be who you are. A mentor will expect you to become the best you can be.

Expecting the best out of others could also mean that people like the way they see themselves when they look at themselves through *your* eyes. As we have said many times, "Your people need to be able to see *their* victory in *your* eyes." Let's face it. People can go just about anywhere to get dumped on. They can hear negativity and pessimism anywhere. But there are very few places, perhaps none, where they can go to be believed in, uplifted, and encouraged. We need to make sure that those involved in LIFE Leadership know beyond a shadow of a doubt that they have a person or group of people who believe in them and expect the best that they have to give.

It has been said that, "You will discover your true greatness as soon as you begin to *feel* and *see* yourself as a great person." LIFE Leadership is about finding people, identifying their greatness, and showing it to them continually until they begin to see it for themselves. People are the happiest when they live up to the highest expectations they have of themselves. Let's help them *raise* those expectations, *visualize* those expectations, and *realize* those expectations.

Build Relationships

To hold people to highs standards and give them a true, higher picture of themselves, we must first develop a *relationship* with them. As the saying goes, "People don't care how much you know until they know how much you care." We have found no truer maxim when attempting to influence people.

As Tim Marks says, "If you want to help someone, *help them like you first*." What Tim is driving at is that in order to build a relationship, one must become relatable and likeable to other people. This is the reason there is so much emphasis in the LIFE Training Marketing System on people skills. We all come into the industry deficient, to some degree, in this area. And no matter how good we become at dealing with people, we can and should always get better. Another Tim Marks quote is, "Activity minus people skills plus time equals frustration." You can do a lot of work, but without good interactions with people, it will be in vain.

There are those that are chronic overtalkers, while others are painfully shy. Some are too loud, brash, and boastful, while others have annoying habits like interrupting or finishing people's sentences for them. We must all analyze ourselves just a little and reduce our weaknesses while we focus most of our attention on enhancing our strengths. And we must also become good at over-looking those annoying tendencies in others.

An anonymous poem does a good job of succinctly summarizing some very important people skills:

> The six most important words:
> I admit that I was wrong.
> The five most important words:
> You did a great job.
> The four most important words:
> What do you think?
> The three most important words:
> Could you please...?
> The two most important words:

Thank you.
The one most important word:
We.

People skills open the door to relationships. But people skills are just that: *skills*. What has to happen in a relationship is something more, something deeper. There must be caring and sincerity. To build a relationship, we must really connect with the other person. We must find common ground, develop mutual respect, and offer a listening ear. We probably shouldn't resort to another poem so quickly, but we can't resist.

If I Knew You and You Knew Me

If I knew you and you knew me—
If both of us could clearly see,
And with an inner sight divine
The meaning of your heart and mine—
I'm sure that we should differ less
And clasp our hands in friendliness;
Our thoughts would pleasantly agree
If I knew you and you knew me.

If I knew you and you knew me,
As each one knows his own self, we
Could look each other in the face
And see therein a truer grace.
Life has so many hidden woes,
So many thorns for every rose;
The "why" of things our hearts would see,
If I knew you and you knew me.

—Nixon Waterman

To build a relationship with someone is to drive at really knowing that person. When that happens, he or she will give you permission to influence, help, and lead. But nurture such relationships tenderly; they are among the most wonderful "things" on earth.

Before leaving this section, we want to emphasize that the building of relationships is perhaps the most important thing to learn in your entire business journey. Blow this one, and blow it all. Take this lightly, and your business will treat you lightly. Do poorly at this step, and *perfection* in rotating the pattern, listening to audios, showing the plan, or whatever else will produce mediocrity at best. On the other hand, get good at this step, and you can be sloppy at all the others, and things will work out just fine!

Develop Character

There are really two types of abilities when dealing with people, both of which are important. The first is the ability to make a good first impression, what we have elsewhere in this book called relatability. The second is the ability to build deeper and more meaningful relationships with people as they become more familiar with you. For this second category, the pertinent question is: Do people like you more or less as they get to know you better?

At the heart of this second kind of ability with people is the question of *character*. Are we who we say we are? Does our walk match our talk? Phonies will get exposed, sooner or later. As the saying goes, "Always tell the truth; then you won't have to keep track of everything you say." As Abraham Lincoln famously said, "You can fool all of the people some of the time, some of the people all of the time, but not all of the people all of the time."

People who lack character sometimes behave as if they think they are "getting away with it," that somehow others aren't picking up on their deceptions or dishonesty. But this is rarely the case. Lies only hold up for so long, and when they see the light of day, they normally burn through the trust in relationships in a hurry. Once trust is gone, the relationship is in dire jeopardy. Only time, forgiveness, maturity, repentance, personal change, and a host of other benevolences can rebuild what was destroyed.

It is far better to guard our character and build on it daily. As R. C. Samsel said:

Character is the foundation stone upon which one must build to win respect. Just as no worthy building can be erected on a weak foundation, so no lasting reputation worthy of respect can be built on a weak character. Without character, all effort to attain dignity is superficial, and the results are sure to be disappointing.

The best way to build relationships, and your business, is upon a foundation of character. And that foundation is built brick by brick, one day at a time. Build wisely.

Choose Your Responses

When building a business with other people, you must develop the maturity to choose your responses to the little situations that will eventually come up from time to time. That ability to choose based on your emotional intelligence and not your *emotional knee-jerk reaction* will go a long way to developing relationships with others and demonstrating the depth of your character.

There will be occurrences and circumstances that will arise. There will be challenges. It seems that when dealing with people, there is always something amiss. Many times your response to the problem is more important than the problem itself. If you have a tendency to "fly off the handle," "boil over," "pitch a fit," "lose your cool," "come unglued," "get your knickers in knots," "have your tail feathers ruffled," "hit the ceiling," "get your nose out of joint," "bite someone's head off," "give a piece of your mind," "grind your axe," "read them the riot act," "let them have it," "give them what they've got coming to them," "dress them down," "take the gloves off," "tell them a thing or two," "get a load off," "tell them where it's at," "lose control," "tell them where they can—" well, you get the idea, then you will damage relationships and your ability to influence others. A famous adage says, "We are only as big as the smallest thing that upsets us."

Authors Dave Balter and John Butman wrote:

The way a company responds to negative word-of-mouth can create positive word-of-mouth. According to a study by W. Glynn Mangold et al., half of all negative word-of-mouth comes from consumers who feel a sense of injustice about the way they are treated by a company when they have a problem, rather than by the shortcomings in the product or service itself. So, the way a company responds to negative word-of-mouth becomes an important part of the conversation, possibly the most important part of it.

If choosing a proper response is appropriate for a company, certainly it is important for an individual business owner choosing to build a big business, too. You must learn to choose your responses and to choose well.

How do we do this? First, we need to realize that in LIFE Leadership, there really are no emergencies. Nothing is *that* urgent that it's worth "blowing our stack" or "throwing down with someone" or, well, never mind. (Sometimes we just can't help it!) Also, it will be helpful to realize that when people do things that bring us to anger, they probably didn't do them on purpose. It is extremely doubtful that someone would wake up one morning and think, "You know, I think I'll screw up so-and-so's day today. I know just how to hurt his feelings!" Instead, we should be quick to give others the benefit of the doubt and slow to give them the wrath of our shout. Most circumstances turn out to be misunderstandings. If we choose an appropriate, controlled, loving, patient response to the things that occur, we will leave the door open to actually solving the problems at hand.

Give More Than Is Expected

There is a story told of a builder whose son wanted to enter the trade with him. To help him begin, the father allotted $200,000 to the son for the purpose of constructing his first house. Upon the sale of the home on the open market, father and son would split the proceeds. By all accounts, this was a great deal for the son.

Unfortunately, the son's honor was not in line with the father's generosity. Throughout the project, the son cut corners and cheapened the quality of the house in order to make secret profits. By the end of the project, more than $50,000 had been "shaved" in this way from the construction cost of the home. Most of these economies were taken from the structure and foundation of the building where inspectors and generous fathers would not notice. As the project neared completion, the father burst out with happy news: The home was to be a gift to the son! He could keep the house for his own!

Many people go through life giving less than their best. They cut corners and take the easy way out, ignoring the maxim "If there's a job worth doing, it's worth doing right." There seems to be a prevalence in our society today of people giving just enough to get by.

These attitudes will not do. Successful people give their best; in fact, *they give more than is expected,* not less. When this is not the case, it is only a matter of time and circumstance before the "corner cutting" will come back to haunt. As the saying goes, "Those who take short cuts only end up getting cut short." A good rule of thumb is to under promise and over deliver.

Persevere

Just as consistency is paramount to allowing activity to accumulate into long-term results, so too is perseverance. Without the ability to hang in there through "thick and thin," "the good, the bad, and the ugly," "rain or shine," "feast or famine," "sickness or health," "better or worse until death do us part..." (Er, um, okay. No more. We promise this time, really.) Without the ability to persevere, we rob ourselves of the accumulation of our efforts.

This is a failure mode we see with so many people. They just can't make it around the next bend in the road. So many times, success is little more than hanging on long enough for it all to come together for you. Also, the longer you persist in the pursuit of something, the more confidence and determination you will develop.

As Don B. Owens Jr. said, "Many people fail in life because they believe in the adage: If you don't succeed, try something else." We have seen this many times. People will come into the industry, give it a try, and then disappear at the first sign of resistance. They become convinced they've either found something better (the next great thing) or that their old way of living wasn't *that* bad. This is sad. They are basically burning their chances to accomplish their dreams. Not that there aren't other great opportunities out there and not that their life before LIFE Leadership was all bad either, but someone who has no staying power will have no dream-achieving power. Billy Sunday said, "More men fail through lack of purpose than lack of talent." And that lack of purpose shows up in a lack of perseverance.

By the way, when people move on to the "next best thing" or bow out of challenges easily, they don't succeed in other endeavors either. This is because the opportunity wasn't the problem; the *individual* was. As Tim Marks says, "No matter where I go, there I am!" It's like the man whose grandson decides to play a trick on him by smearing Limburger cheese on his moustache as he sleeps. After that, everywhere the grandfather goes that day, he says, "This room smells!" When he decides to go outside for some fresh air, he says, "It smells out here, too!" After a while, he's convinced that *everything* smells! Indeed, if we are the problem, then wherever we go, we'll encounter the same problem all over again. To improve, we must remember: "The best way to accelerate one's success is to double one's failure rate." When people quit after a setback, they stop the process. This teaches nothing. They start again, as it were, at zero. When the next obstacle comes up, it's time to quit again, and the whole cycle starts over. All the while, they are missing the best education of all: the one that comes from failing, getting up, getting better, and trying again, over and over.

There is a way to encourage perseverance, and that is to realize that all results are not visible on the outside. While it may look to outside observers that you are making no progress, there is a different story about what is happening *within* you. Many times, success requires *internal* growth long before any *external* growth shows up. This was especially true for us. As we began our first business ventures, we were quite sure we'd be successful. But it took a lot of listening to audios, reading books, and attending seminars and associating with other like-minded business owners, including very special mentors, for us to experience the internal changes that eventuated in the external changes.

Perseverance is also served by staying focused on one's *dreams*. It is not any particular business we stay committed to through good times and bad, but rather our dreams. We were shown a diagram a long time ago that depicted this:

What is shown here is that an individual's dreams aren't big enough, so they can't be seen. All that can be seen are the obstacles. The following diagram demonstrates what is necessary to fuel our perseverance and propel us to succeed: in essence, making sure our dreams are bigger than the obstacles!

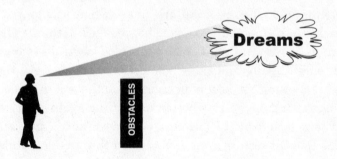

By the way, this can also be accomplished by making one's self bigger than the obstacles. This is the very reason for LIFE Training's vast array of training materials!

We will leave this discussion on perseverance with this quote from speaker and author Denis Waitley: "Success is almost totally dependent upon drive and persistence. The extra energy required to make another effort or try another approach is the secret of winning."

Fall in Love with Learning

We will close this chapter with an admonition that one of the most important principles for success is the desire to learn, and to learn continuously. Bill Belichick, record-setting head coach of the New England Patriots, has achieved success few in his field can match. The secret, according to author David Halberstam, is that at an early stage in his career, Belichick decided to *fall in love with learning*. That's what has to happen for success in anything, really. One has to have a burning desire to learn more and more so one can get better and better.

As the ancient Greek writer Euripides wrote, "We must take care of our minds because we cannot benefit from beauty when our brains are missing." (We don't care who you are; that right there is funny.) And as Henry Ford said, "Anyone who stops learning is old, whether at twenty or eighty. Anyone who keeps learning stays young." We would add that anyone who keeps learning keeps his or her business growing, too. So develop the love of learning and never stop. Hit the LIFE Training Marketing System with a passion. Listen to audios and watch videos over and over, read books, attend every event, and seek mentorship. As Charlie Jones said, "You are the same today that you are going to be five years from now except for two things: the people with whom you associate and the books you read."

Whatever format is used, it is important to continually reinforce the principles.
—James Hunter

If you think the people you attract could be better, then it's time for you to improve yourself.
—John Maxwell

Our privileges are not for our pleasure. Rather, they are for a higher purpose, to serve others.
—Chris Brady

Leaders haven't simply practiced their vocation or profession. They've mastered it.
—Warren Bennis

Do what you can, with what you have, where you are.
—Theodore Roosevelt

Name: CORPORATE CARTER
Quote: "This all sounds quite
        feasible, but I'm afraid it might
        create a conflict of interest
        with my job. I'm next in line for
        the Executive III position that's
        opening up in HR next quarter,
        and I would hate to jeopardize
        my promotion."

CHAPTER 11

BUSINESS OWNERSHIP
THE SPECIFICS

The elements discussed in the previous chapter are primarily *principles* of success. They apply to LIFE Leadership but are also required in any worthy endeavor. This chapter will be different in that it will focus on *specifics* of building a community of LIFE Members.

Edification

In the LIFE Training system, you will hear the word *edification* used a lot. Webster's Dictionary defines edifying as, "building up, establishing, or instructing and improving." When you hear the word used in connotation with LIFE Leadership, it is being applied to *people*. One of the most important specifics of building LIFE Leadership is the concept of edifying other people—in effect, building them up or improving them with your words.

This is perhaps a foreign concept in our world of pessimism, gossip, backstabbing, and sarcasm. People in general society seem to take special pleasure in tearing into other people with their words. This is unfortunate because few people seem to realize the power of the words they say, especially if they are negative. Negativity, it appears, is many times stronger than positivity.

It is for this reason that we must learn to speak well of one another. By this, we don't mean some false form of flattery or anything insincere. We believe that with a little practice and a good heart, anyone can learn to see the good in other people. Edifying others means finding out the good about them and putting it into words. You might be surprised, perhaps, by how powerful a kind word to or about someone can be. We have all heard the saying "If you can't think of something good to say, don't say anything at all." But we believe even this little statement can be improved. "If you can't think of something good to say, you'd better think harder. There is *almost always* something good to say."

You've perhaps heard also that it's impolite to talk "behind someone's back." We disagree. We think it's extremely important to be talking behind people's backs, that is, as long as the talk is positive and complimentary. Imagine how endearing you'd become to someone if he or she found out that you had been singing his or her praises all over town!

There is a reason for edification of other people that goes beyond the mere fact that it is the right thing to do (and therefore should be done anyway). LIFE Leadership, as we've said many times, is a business of working with people. Edification becomes the grease that helps all the gears work harmoniously together without grinding.

For instance, imagine how effective a person in your upline would be if you were to provide proper edification before he or she met with people in your organization. If you inform your organization of your upline's accomplishments, as well as the specific things he or she has done to help you, then chances are your organization will be much more receptive to and respectful of everything that particular upline has to say. In this way, by building up your upline through the process of edification, you are giving him or her more power to be effective in your group. It is natural for people to think, "Why should I listen to this person?" Edification can answer that question and open their ears.

Additionally, imagine what a harmonious community of people you would build if you taught everyone to edify each other all the time. In effect, what you would be doing is "good-finding" each other. Such an environment would be energizing, positive, comfortable, and endearing. And those are the exact kinds of words people have used to describe the environment at LIFE Leadership's various seminars and meetings across the country. "There's just something different about you," they say. "It's just something you can feel in the air." A big part of that "feeling" is that LIFE Members have learned to edify and encourage each other.

Edification cannot be mechanical. It can't be something that you do because you know that you are supposed to. Rather, it must be true and sincere. It must come from the heart. We must all become good at finding the good in others. If we have trouble doing this, perhaps we have issues with our pride that we need to address.

One of our favorite quotes is by Harry Truman: "You would be surprised how much you could accomplish if you didn't care who got the credit." Edification is about giving credit away. Build others up so that they can be more effective and perhaps even help you in return.

Someone once asked if edification might be lying. After all, saying good things about people is choosing to ignore the "less than good things" that could be said about any of us. Is this an error of omission? The answer is no. There is nothing wrong with choosing to see the good in people. Edification is the art of identifying an individual's strengths and then "packaging" that person properly. A person's strengths should be put in the right light; he or she should not be attributed with false strengths. In building the business, one needs to have the proper "package" for each of his or her upline business partners in order to appropriately edify them based on the strengths they bring to building the team.

Duplication

We already touched on duplication a few times earlier in this book. We couldn't help it. That's because duplication is such a big part of what makes the LIFE Training Marketing System so effective in helping to build communities.

When LIFE Leadership is built properly, Members are plugged into the training system. That training system becomes their source of information. They learn to listen to audios and watch videos to answer their questions. They learn to read books to improve themselves. And they attend seminars and Leadership Conventions to get inspired, get recognized, and learn the information that will be vital in helping them move on. The key here is that the *system* becomes their source, *not* the upline Member. If a LIFE Member builds his or her team properly by plugging everyone entirely into the training system, then that LIFE Member has developed what Robert Kiyosaki calls a B-type business. This is a situation in which a *system* runs the business instead of the *owner*. Why is this important? Precisely because the concept of wealth is not just money; it must also be accompanied by enough free time to enjoy that money. When LIFE Members build businesses properly founded in the LIFE Training system, they set themselves up not only for income but for time to enjoy it as well.

Duplication also sets up a pattern where, after a while, the business grows without the direct input of the business owner. In the beginning, the business owner must show every plan, find every customer, and move every ticket. But eventually, other people copy that LIFE Member's example and begin doing the work also. This is duplication. And as we stated earlier, the better the example, the better the duplication. If they build their businesses properly, using the strategies of depth and the LIFE Training Marketing System, Members will eventually see them spread to people they have never met and to geographic locations to which they have never been. This can develop into geometric, outward growth. This is the power of compounding at its best. It is at this point that the LIFE Member has a true B-type business and begins getting some of his or her time back.

Because of the multiplication possible through the structure of the LIFE Leadership Compensation Plan, it is important for a Member to think about the concept of duplication in everything he or she does. At every turn, the Member should ask, "Is this duplicable? Would I want a thousand people doing what I'm about to do?"

There have been many LIFE Members who have decided to do things "their way." They get a crazy notion here or put a twist on things there and wonder why their business isn't growing. Or they wonder why their whole team is so off track. Being just a little off track at the beginning of the journey can result in arriving miles away from the target further on.

There is another way to explain this. In *The Cashflow Quadrant,* Robert Kiyosaki compares the poor and the middle class to the wealthy. One of the chief differences between them is how they generate their income. The poor and the middle class are taught that it is all about *them*. They must be effective, smart, educated, capable, and indispensable. Whereas, the wealthy realize it should not be about them at all, eventually. Wealth comes from a *system* that runs a business. The person becomes less and less a factor in the equation as success mounts and wealth streams in systematically. This cannot happen if the business is built upon the individual's constant inputs, tweaks, and adjustments or if the person is indispensable to the income on an ongoing basis. In effect, the wealthy take themselves out of the picture and let systematic income generation become the whole picture. The poor and the middle class try to make *themselves* the whole picture.

Understanding this concept, we can then see the extreme importance of making sure that everything we do is duplicatable and systematic. The more of "us" that we pump into it, the more of "us" that will be required to generate the income and the less systematic it will be. Again, look at the master copy. Always make sure it is worth duplicating and, therefore, will generate systematic success.

Promotion

Promotion is the ability to encourage others to take steps in the business that will be beneficial to them, specifically the steps of getting involved in the LIFE Training system. Let's face it. People are programmed to try to get by on minimums. "What's the least I can do and get the most out of it?" "How little can I pay for it?" etc. But success doesn't work that way. No pain, no gain. No investment, no return.

In LIFE Leadership, one of the great advantages is that the expenses and investments required are laughably low. On any kind of scale compared to any kind of conventional business, the amount of money that is required to build LIFE Leadership doesn't even show up! But because this industry is unconventional, people often don't evaluate their investments in it as investments. Instead, they begin to think of them as expenses. A painter who pays thousands of dollars for equipment will hesitate when it comes to buying an audio. A lawyer who has tens of thousands of dollars invested into his education and accreditations will baulk at subscribing to the seminars! The ability to overcome these natural tendencies of the uninformed and help them become informed is what we call promotion.

Promotion is accomplished by helping others see the LIFE Training system's stack of benefits. You have to help them see the value in investing. In the words we've used before, you have to help them understand "what's in it for them." This involves showing them the relevance of why they should attend that next event or get involved with the Marketing System.

One way to do this is to tie whatever is being promoted to the other person's dream. Help him or her see how taking the appropriate steps in the business relates to accomplishing the dream(s) that got him or her interested in LIFE Leadership in the first place.

Another approach involves matching the promotion to the person. If you know that the person to whom you are promoting something is a detailed individual, be sure and explain the details he or she will be receiving from attending that seminar. If the person is a fun-seeking "people person," be sure and promote the large crowd that will be there and all the fun that will be had. If someone is casual, easy-going, and soft-spoken, let that person know you really want him or her to go and that you are looking forward to spending time together. The final type of person, the aggressive type, should be told that all the leaders will be there! When promoting to specific personality types, be sincere. Don't play games. Just help them see which part of the event or tool is the most relevant for their particular temperament.

It all comes down to creating a hunger on the part of others. You must try to show them what is in it for them and why it will have relevance. It is important that they feel that you are trying to help them, not to sell them on something. Be sure and establish rapport and show them that you care. If they come up with objections, take the time to work through them, in much the same way as we discussed in the section on following through. Belief, conviction, and excitement on your part will carry the day. Promotion requires posture, just like everything else in this industry. It isn't important that *they* believe; it's only important that they believe that *you* believe in it. Once they experience things for themselves, they will believe, too! If not, at least you did your part and "got them to the campfire." If they don't like the roasted marshmallows, at least you got them there to discover that for themselves.

We don't want participants in the LIFE Training Marketing System incurring any unnecessary expenses. Remember, they are in LIFE Leadership to make some money. We must always be trying to help them accomplish that. What we are interested in helping them do is invest wisely for the best possible return on investment. If they are not going to use what you are trying to promote, then by all means, do not promote it! Remember the axiom we've been referring back to throughout this book: *What's in it for them?* Always keep that in mind, and your promotion will be spot on.

Promotion is absolutely essential to building a big business. As one successful business owner once said, "You must get good at promoting in order to have a big business. And if you're not good at promoting, you'll have a big business once you get good at promoting!"

Mentors

There are two sure ways to failure: (1) listening to everyone and (2) listening to no one. The route to success is somewhere in between. Personal experience is certainly an effective teacher, but trial and error can be painful and is always slower than learning from someone else. However, no one person is infallible, and nobody has all the answers. Therefore, following a single individual can be narrowing at best, dangerous at worst. What is best is to find a multitude of counselors (as the Bible recommends) that are like-minded and unified in their message. They will still have differing personalities, perspectives, and experiences, but their information and experiences can be invaluable to others traversing the same path. The LIFE Training Marketing System provides access to exactly that type of "unified diversity." Every speaker on a LIFE Leadership stage, or on a recording, has achieved success to a level high enough to warrant his or her invitation to present experiences and knowledge to others. The range of teachers in the Marketing System is extremely diverse. But the message and information these achievers share is right on track. It works. And it can work for others who learn what these people have learned and do what they have done.

Finding and listening to mentors is one of the most misunderstood, unknown, and overlooked parts of success. Most of us can think back to someone in our lives who had a special impact on us: hopefully a parent but also maybe a teacher, relative, or coach. That person might have seen more in us than we had previously seen in ourselves. Maybe he or she expected the best out of us and wouldn't listen to our excuses. Those types of people in our lives, in a way, were early mentors.

Professional success of the highest kind, and especially in this industry, requires mentorship. Mentorship is the process of utilizing the experience of someone who has achieved the results you want. As the saying goes, "The best route to success is in the footsteps of someone who has gone before you."

In all business, there is a mine field of things that can happen between initial excitement and success. A mentor becomes your tour guide through that mine field. What is the best way to learn? Through experience—*other people's* experience. That's the role of a mentor: to provide that experience.

So a key thing to know when building a community is that you are going to want to seek out mentorship. At first, this will probably be limited to the training materials in the system. It might also include the person or persons who were involved in getting you started. But as you perform, you will get noticed by those in the upline and begin to qualify for special meetings and even one-on-one time with your upline leadership. Take advantage of these situations! One great piece of advice or perspective from someone who has prospered in LIFE Leadership might be just the nugget you need to move on!

Over time, it will become obvious to you who your main mentor in the business will be. There isn't any hard-and-fast rule about this. There is nothing formalized. But this is good because as a result, you may have the privilege of having several mentors as you rise up through the levels of success. This is one factor that sets our industry apart. In much of corporate America, mentorship is not even talked about, much less practiced. But here, it is a way of life.

As you get time around those who have gone further than you in the business, take advantage of it. Have your questions ready. And be ready to listen. Many times, people think that time with their mentor is a chance to blab about all that they've been doing. Chances are your mentor already *knows* how you've been doing. He or she is fully aware of the measurements of your business that we talked about in chapter nine. The purpose of meeting with your mentor is primarily to *gain perspective*. Remember that how you see things is critical. Your upline mentor can help you see in the correct light. He or she will be able to help you make sense of things you haven't seen or understood before and can help reframe your challenges so that you see them in the most advantageous way.

Another thing to keep in mind when communicating with your mentor is to do your own thinking. What we mean by this is that you should think about your challenges and obstacles and come up with your own conclusions. Then bounce those off your mentor to check the quality of your thinking on the subject. "Am I seeing this correctly? Am I thinking about this right? Here's what's happening, and here's what I think I've got to do about it. What do you think?" This is the correct way to take the most advantage of your mentor's experience.

Be careful when dealing with your mentor to be open and honest. We all want to look good. We all want to impress those for whom we have the most respect. But don't just show up and "put on a good face." Don't say "I know" to everything your mentor recommends. It's okay *not* to know. That's why you've pursued a mentor in the first place, so that you could learn to know what you didn't even know you didn't know.

Conversely, don't show up and "dump" on your mentor. He or she is not there to hear a bunch of complaints and whining. A mentor wants to deal with people who are committed to success, honest about their current abilities, and hungry to improve. This will require clear, honest communication.

The subject of mentorship is enormous, and interestingly, it is very lightly treated in popular success literature. That is one reason we wrote the book *Launching a Leadership Revolution*. In its pages, we deal with the subject of mentorship in detail. It may be helpful for you to read those sections to gain a deeper understanding of what you should be seeking from your mentors. The book *Mentoring Matters* from the LIFE Leadership Essentials Series can also be very helpful in this area. But suffice it to say that seeking, finding, and utilizing a mentor is fundamental to achieving the highest levels of success.

Counsel Upline

This topic goes along with what we said above about seeking and utilizing a mentor. The phrase "counsel upline" is most often used to indicate the value of free advice. In the business world outside of this industry, trade secrets and strategies are closely guarded. Cards are held close to the chest. Everything is competitive, and there is very little sharing of information that could jeopardize a successful enterprise by enabling competitors. But in LIFE Leadership, those who have gone before you and have gained experience and success actually benefit from sharing their secrets with you. For this reason, each of us has individuals in our upline who are more successful than we are in the business yet are accessible to us. These are the mentors of whom we spoke before.

We often recommend that LIFE Members counsel upline before taking actions in the business about which they are unsure. It is also recommended that all major purchases be run past the upline before making them. This is where people sometimes get confused. "Do I have to ask permission to be able to buy something?" Certainly not. Each Member runs his or her own business and is free to do whatever he or she wants to do, within the rules. Counseling upline is not asking for permission; it is asking for free advice. Think back to the times in your life where you chose poorly in some circumstances. What would the value have been of having someone in your life with a vested interest in your well-being you could have consulted beforehand? The answer? Priceless. That's what your upline can provide: priceless perspective and advice that you can then choose to follow or not.

It's a good idea to counsel upline any time you feel like "tweaking the system" or modifying the pattern, even in the slightest ways. That's because, chances are, your innovation has already been tried, and your more experienced upline can shed light on what occurred and why it may or may not be a good idea. Additionally, if your idea is a good one, your upline can take it to his or her upline, and ultimately, it can get taught across the entire team, which only helps everyone!

Cross-Lining

Imagine that you invested years of effort into raising your son. You were there when he took his first steps, you taught him how to throw a ball, and you had "the talk" with him about the birds and the bees. Then imagine that some other person started taking your son aside and teaching him things that were *your responsibility* to teach him. Imagine that this person, who had no authority to do so, even taught things that were in conflict with the values you had worked so hard to instill in your child. (And no, we are not trying to bash colleges here, but...) How would that make you feel?

We use that example as a way to introduce the subject of cross-lining in the community building industry because cross-lining is one of those topics that are almost impossible to understand until they happen to you. What is meant by cross-lining in the business is very near the example we just gave, except replace "your son" in the example with "a Member in your organization."

We are not sure why it happens. Maybe it's some odd corner of human nature. But people like to stick their noses where they don't belong. That's the beginning of cross-lining. Somebody in a different organization, a "cross-line" organization (hence the term), begins building a relationship or sharing information with someone who is in neither his or her upline nor his or her downline.

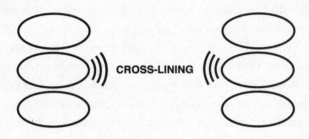

When this happens, nothing good can come from it. There is always a damaging result.

Here's an example. Let's say two cross-line LIFE Members strike up a conversation out in the hall at an Open Meeting. One Member says to the other, "How's it going?" to which the other replies, "Great! It's growing faster than ever!" This might seem like a pretty harmless interchange. But what if the first Member isn't experiencing rapid business growth at the moment? He or she walks away thinking, "What's wrong with *me*? Why isn't my business growing as fast as *his business*? Actually, what's wrong with my upline? Maybe if I were on *his* team instead of the one I'm on, *my business* would be growing faster, too." We've seen this happen time and again. The other thing that this interchange could cause is doubt on the part of the faster growing Member. He or she might walk away from that exchange thinking, "Wow. That person doesn't seem to be doing too well. Maybe I'm just getting lucky right now with my business growth. Maybe it won't last." We agree. The conclusions these two fictional characters are making are overblown, short-term, uninformed, and incorrect. But people don't always have the discernment to see this for themselves, especially when they are the ones in the situation.

A worse type of cross-lining is the intentional kind. This is where, normally, a LIFE Member has been in the business a while and begins feeling comfortable. He or she thinks the rules of cross-lining somehow don't apply to *him or her*. So the person starts "chatting up" every cross-line Member he or she can. He or she might even be bold enough to start asking for business advice or private business information. "Say, how did your PBO count do this month?" or "So how many people have you guys got here at this seminar?" or "How are you guys contacting people?" This is a very poisonous situation and should be stopped immediately. Why? Because it is impolite, it's unfair to the upline who have worked with and invested time into those people, and it's just not any of the inquiring person's business (literally).

Social networking sites on the Internet have proliferated in recent times, and these have become wonderful tools for connecting with others and staying in touch. However, in the case of minding one's own business and refraining from cross-lining, they can become very damaging. At the risk of stating the obvious, the entire concept of etiquette and minding one's own business ought to be applied to the world of social networking, too.

Now don't get us wrong. The idea of cross-lining doesn't mean you can't talk to people that are not on your team. It doesn't mean you can't be part of the camaraderie that being around cross-line organizations provides. It doesn't mean you have to be uptight and act weird around people who are not part of your upline or down-line organization. But what it does mean is that you should keep your interactions appropriate. Show respect to the people that are mentoring those business owners. Be a team player. And actually, be more focused on your own team than on somebody else's. Taking it back to the example we started this section with: raise your own kids!

There is another aspect of cross-lining that we should point out. Those that grow the fastest, biggest businesses simply don't have time for it. They are too involved serving their own team and working with their own business partners to have time to mess with anybody else's. It has been our experience that we don't have all the time we would like to spend with each of the partners on our own teams as it is, much less get involved with those who are not on our teams.

Communication in our type of business should always be within the personal sponsorship tree. That means either upline or downline. Communication with cross-line LIFE Members should be friendly, encouraging, and appropriate. Enough said.

Negative Upline

There is another little specific to this profession that we should now explain, and thankfully, it is easier to explain than cross-lining! This is the concept that when you have something "negative" to say, that you say it *upline* and not *downline*. You might be amazed at how often people find something negative to say and then run out and tell their group about it. This does nothing but cause doubt and consternation in their team. It's like spewing poison onto a plant you're trying to grow!

Instead, if you have an issue or something that is less than positive and uplifting, take it upline. Chances are they can handle it. More important, they will know how to help you handle it. And remember, it's not "negative" (i.e. "whining" and "complaining") if you come truly seeking a *solution*.

Goal Setting

To make sure you are productive in the business and not simply busy, it will be important to make goal setting a part of your business habits. Here is a brief excerpt from *Launching a Leadership Revolution* on this concept:

> In the words of the hockey great Wayne Gretzky, "You will miss 100% of the shots you don't take." We must assume he was referring to shots on a *goal*. Without specific goals at which to direct our energies and ambitions, our efforts will be wandering generalities at best....
>
> The story is told of two men who set out to accomplish similar results. One invested the effort to properly set

goals and the other did not. At the end of a period of time, both men had worked diligently, but the one who had set a specific goal by far outperformed the other man. This is because everything the goal-setting man did was unconsciously directed toward his goal. If there was something to be done, it was first determined if it would assist him in accomplishing his goal. If it would, then he did it. If it would not help him hit his goal, he would not do it. You see, the goal-setting man had the advantage of priorities over the non-goal-setting man. He also had the advantage of channeling his efforts more effectively through the power of focus. On any given day there are a number of "good" things to be done, but there are only a few "great" things to be done. And there can only be one "best" thing to do. A leader knows and does the "best" things on a regular basis.

Like with hunger, goal setting is a discipline. It should never be a haphazard affair....There are several components to the proper setting of goals that every leader should embody.

Goals must:

1. Be Specific
2. Be Written
3. Be Set in Stone
4. Be Measurable
5. Be Realistic
6. Provide Motivation
7. Be in Line with Priorities and Values
8. Be Prominent
9. Have a Specific Time Period

Proper goal setting coincides with the measurements we talked about in chapter nine. How many plans are you going to show this month? How many levels deep do you plan on going in your taproot organization? What will your PBO count be? How many per each leg? What will your product volume be? What about your customer volume? Remember to keep things in the order of conquer (plans shown and depth built), fortify (people on system), and domesticate (product volume and subscriptions). And don't set too many goals or get too complicated about it. It is useless to focus on many things at once. For most of us, we find that we do better when we focus upon one main goal at a time. All the other goals that align with it will fall into place eventually if we hit the main goal.

Another goal to consider is taking part in the various customer sales contests that LIFE Leadership holds from time to time. For instance, there is almost always an individual sales contest in which top sales performers are awarded cash prizes, recognition onstage, and sometimes even dream trips. These usually involve rewards to several finishers, so don't think that you don't have a chance of winning. Set an appropriate goal for your customer base, and go for it! In addition to individual sales contests, there is also a top sales team contest. Find out which upline couple would be representing your team onstage if your team were to win that particular competition. This is a group contest and involves the entire team. The way it works is that every retail sale of every product to every customer for the entire team during the period between Leadership Conventions counts toward the contest. So every sale you make counts! This is a particularly fun competition because everyone on a team can participate, and it builds great camaraderie and memories.

So set goals each month, counsel with your upline mentor(s) about them, and run for them with all you've got. If you should miss a goal, reset it and try again. You will get better and better at goal setting as you gain experience. You will learn the futility of setting goals too high and the impotence of setting goals too low. Goals set too high will discourage you. Conversely, goals set too low will not motivate you.

Money Management

There is a slightly humorous saying that rings true: "The only way to get wealthy is to make more than you spend and also to spend less than you earn." This is only too simple. But almost nobody follows it.

In our years in this industry, we have seen countless people get involved because they need to make more money. So far so good. But after a while, the reason they need to make more money becomes obvious: *they waste the money they make.*

A common fallacy in people's minds goes something like this, "Well, I'll be out of all this money trouble as soon as I start making more money. That's why I joined LIFE Leadership." And to a degree, that is a correct statement. However, it is not a correct statement if the person has no *discipline* in handling his or her finances. Read the following statement very carefully: **If you do not develop financial discipline and self-control, you will never be wealthy, no matter how much money you make.** Making more money is never the solution to someone in this condition. Why, you might ask? Because a *lack of money* is not the *problem*; therefore, an *increase in money* cannot be the *solution*. A *lack of discipline* is the problem. Therefore, only an *increase in discipline* can be the solution.

For this reason, the LIFE Training Marketing System focuses a lot on developing self-discipline and maturity. The system also talks about money and its proper management. In fact, it might be fair to say that the LIFE Training system will require you to get and continue an education in four categories:

1. Business particulars
2. Success principles
3. People
4. Money

To begin with, being irresponsible with money is downright dishonest. If you write a check to someone, the moment you sign your name, you are in effect giving your word that the money is *there* and immediately available. Bouncing a check is the same as lying. Now we understand that banks and people make mistakes, and we've probably all had the occasion upon which an error caused a bounced check. But that's not what we're talking about here. We're talking about dishonesty, and far too many people have somehow gotten it into their heads that bouncing checks is "acceptable." It is not. There is no excuse.

People waste their money in all sorts of different ways, as we'll demonstrate in the next section. To succeed financially, both husband and wife must learn to live on less than they earn. Period. This may involve cutting back on the number of restaurant visits, canceling the cable television or the extra channels, or beginning to live on a budget. This is a critical area in which to counsel with your upline and determine how you have been doing to this point. Your upline can provide a game plan to help you maximize what you are getting out of your current income and make sure you plug the holes.

Here is why this is necessary, and it is a mindset that the average person out there doesn't seem to understand: Money is your slave. It will do exactly what you tell it to do. If you want it to fill you with junk food for the body or junk food for the mind, it will do so perfectly. However, if you can be taught to use your money for *productive* things, your money will actually go out and bring you back *more* money! Too often, people waste their money when they should be leveraging it by putting it to work for them. With LIFE Leadership, people have found a way they can plant seeds of a future financial harvest. Most of these seeds involve the planting of time. But some amount of investment money along the way will be necessary, even though it is quite small when compared to conventional businesses and their capital requirements. Learn to treat money with respect and don't waste it.

On the detail side of things, upon starting your business, you should immediately open up a new and separate checking account. After all, you are running a business now, and it should be treated as such. It should have its own separate finances. Put your income from your business into that account, and draw your expenses for your business from that account. This will make things easier at tax time, also. To start your business, you will need to fund it. Put a chunk of money in that account to get started. If possible, make sure it is enough that you can invest properly in tools, events, sample products, and any other little expenses that might accrue along the way.

Also, keep good records. Keep track of miles driven and keep all receipts for anything incurred while in the honest pursuit of a profit. Tools, travel, products to demonstrate, etc. are all usually deductible expenses. We are not accountants, but we have several very good ones we use as our advisors and tax specialists and preparers. You should, too. Let your tax specialists advise you.

Another category of money management is how to spend your money as it starts to come rolling in as a result of your efforts. The best idea is to set a business goal. Then when you hit that goal, assuming you have also hit a corresponding financial goal (again, counsel upline), you can purchase that item or trip as a reward. That way, each reward you earn through your business becomes a yardstick that measures how many people you have helped along the way. Just avoid the damaging temptation to make the reward greater than the financial reward directly related to the goal. Buying things you can't yet afford simply because you hit a minimum business goal would be directionally incorrect. This is where your financial discipline comes to the rescue.

Your money should ultimately get split in several directions: the money you give away, the money you save, the money you invest, and the money on which you live. There are many great books in our system that delve into this area of learning how to manage and leverage your finances that can help you determine the proper proportion for you for each of these categories. Just remember, money should work for *you*; you should not work for *it*. Waste it, and you'll be its slave. Deploy it wisely, and it'll be yours.

Investment vs. Expense

There is a big difference between *spending* money and *investing* money. Once money is spent, it is gone forever. Money invested, however, should bring a return. To go the farthest in life financially, one should put as much money as possible into investing and as little as possible into spending. Unfortunately, people generally live in the exact opposite way.

Allow us to illustrate with a fun example. You will get more out of this if you play along, and you'll probably enjoy it. (We certainly did.) In the spaces that follow, mark down the average monthly amount you spent (before you got involved in business) on each of the items listed. For things that you purchased perhaps only once or twice a year, divide the one-time purchase cost by twelve months, and write down the average monthly cost of that item. Total your numbers at the bottom.

Before getting exposed to LIFE Leadership, how much money do you estimate that you spent *per month* on each of the following items?

1. Cable or satellite television _____
2. Movie rentals _____
3. Newspaper subscriptions _____
4. Magazine subscriptions _____
5. Music CDs/Downloads _____
6. DVDs/Downloads _____
7. Website subscriptions/shopping _____
8. Cups of coffee _____
9. Bottled water, soft drinks, etc. _____
10. Snacks at a gas station, etc. _____
11. Seeing a movie at a theatre _____
12. Attending a sporting event _____
13. Attending a concert _____
14. Car audio equipment _____
15. Home audio equipment _____
16. Home video equipment _____
17. Restaurant meals, including tips _____
18. Cigarettes _____
19. Alcohol _____
20. Sports league participation _____
21. Other hobbies, golf, etc. _____
22. Any other general recreation _____
23. Video games/equipment _____

Grand Total Average Monthly Expenditure _____

We could conceivably continue this list indefinitely, but we'll stop with that. How did you do? Is your total surprising? It is for most people. We were shocked at the amount of money we were blowing monthly without really realizing it, and worse, without really *accomplishing anything*!

Most of the items in that list are not bad in and of themselves. In fact, most of us enjoy nearly all of them. But it is the accumulated total amount of money we are wasting that should shock us awake. Most people squander a great portion of their income on things they only *sort of want* and, therefore, never accomplish their dreams, the things they *really want* in life.

The principle of investing is best served by the farmer's creed: never eat your seed wheat. Too many people blow what power money could provide by spending it on things that don't get them anywhere.

As you become more and more involved in building your business, it will be important for you to resist the urge to "nickel and dime" it. Remember, LIFE Leadership is built on duplication, and the only way to achieve wealth and freedom is to develop a business where the *system* runs it instead of you. This will require that you plant some "seed wheat," in this case, tools (audios, videos, books, pamphlets, etc.) that can be planted in the lives of people, including yourself.

First of all, don't get confused when you subscribe to the LIFE Training Marketing System or buy tickets to a seminar by thinking that you are *spending* money. You are *investing*, not spending. It strikes us as strange, but we've seen people who have taken the above test and realized they were wasting a couple thousand dollars a month on items that weren't getting them ahead, but those same people baulk at the price of gaining a true education through LIFE Leadership! The first place to invest your money is *yourself*! Any audio, video, or book you need or any conference you need to attend is an investment in *you*. There can be no better investment. You are worth at least as much as all those needless items in the list above. What is more important? Soft drinks and cable television, or improving your mind?

Second, don't be cheap when it comes to planting seeds. If you want a good harvest, you must have a good stock of seeds to plant. Tools on hand are seeds you plant in the lives of other people to grow your business. You will hear talk of something called a "tool trunk." This is the stock of tools any serious business owner should have in his or her car (hence trunk) for the purpose of distributing to potential customers and possible future LIFE Members. A true business owner should have the right amount of tools to allow him or her to do the job correctly. Picture a carpenter who frames homes for a living. Imagine him showing up to the job site with less than an adequate supply of tools. "Can I borrow your nail gun? Are you using that level? Hey buddy, can I strap on your tool belt for a while?" It doesn't happen. Equally silly is a community builder who has an incomplete stock of tools in his or her car. Professionals show up prepared.

A proper stock of tools ought to include at least the following:

1. First-night materials, flip charts, and sketchpads
2. CD packs 2 through 10
3. "Who Do You Know?" brochures
4. Registration forms and "LIFE Leadership Compensation Plan and Income Disclosure Statement" brochures
5. "Next Step Program" brochures
6. Copies of the Top 5 Books
7. Sales aid brochures (including the LIFE Leadership Product Portfolio and the "3 for FREE Program" flyer)
8. Sample products
9. Extra individual CDs (teaching and story types)
10. Board and easel
11. DVDs
12. Copies of this textbook

How much of each is enough? That will be based upon your activity level and desire. The faster you want to go, the better your trunk should be stocked. It's much cheaper to invest in a few tools than it is to meet a quality prospective Member and be short the one thing that might have made the difference in involving that person in your business! So be a professional and stock up. This applies to the products you'll need for advertising and/or handing out to prospects as well as to the stock you'll need with which to get people started.

Next, go out and make those tools work for you. Everywhere you go, create opportunities to hand out materials to prospects and to your team. Obviously, showing a bunch of plans will begin this process, as that will require copies of the *First Night Pack* and then additional materials as you guide people into your business. But never underestimate the need your partners have for the correct information and inspiration, and be sure to promote tools to them every chance you get.

Understand the difference between investment and expense, and maximize your investments while minimizing your expenses. Then make the system work for you.

Husband-and-Wife Teams

Building your business will present many wonderful opportunities to you, in essence, "opportunities within the opportunity." One of these will be the chance to work in close harmony with your spouse.

Okay, so that may or may not excite you yet. But rest assured; many have found that this endeavor becomes a wonderful point of commonality between marriage partners. Where perhaps lives were diverging before, being in business can be something that brings a family closer together.

This may take time, however. It's natural for two people to "warm up" to ideas at different rates. For many couples, one of the individuals in the couple was ready for marriage before the other. Quite possibly, it was the same with having children. LIFE Leadership is no different. Normally, one of the spouses "sees it," and the other spouse eventually agrees to come along, too. In this situation, it is important that the excited spouse doesn't "push" or pressure the non-interested spouse. Just remain positive, get your business working, and applaud any steps the uninvolved spouse takes to help. Given this kind of space, both spouses almost always get up to speed and get excited.

Next, you get to learn to work together as a team! One of the most important teams you will have to build in your business is the *husband-and-wife team*. This will require you to use all the people skills you're learning in the business on *each other* (a novel idea). Many times, people ask us, "What is my role in our business?" The answer to this is that there aren't any solid rules on what the husband does and what the wife does. The only answer is, "Whatever it takes so that the two of you get your business growing." That may sound oversimplified, but the fact is that it is much more important to ask about *attitudes* than it is to ask about *roles*. If you each have the attitude that you will do your part to make your business grow, whatever that is at any given point in time, then your business will do just fine. You'll eventually fall into roles that work the best for both of you within your husband-and-wife team. Along the way, you will find that you have "gotten it together, together."

Building as a Single

So what if your spouse never gets involved, or what if you don't have a spouse? In either of these cases, you will have the chance to build a business as a single. There are some benefits to this, of course (for one, you get to make all decisions about how to spend the money), as well as some differences.

Building a business as a single will require you to cover all aspects of your business yourself, obviously. This means you will need to be sure and be organized and deal properly with the *details* of your business (tracking PBO counts, product volume, setting up customers, etc.), but also be charging ahead in the growth parts of your business (rotating the Five-Step Pattern, and so on). You will essentially be wearing multiple hats. This is okay because we've seen time and time again individuals who have built big businesses as singles, whether male or female, married or unmarried.

There are a few things to be aware of as you build a business as a single. One is to be very businesslike and make sure the impression isn't accidentally made that would suggest your "contact" is anything other than business. The other is to talk about your upline a lot, which will help to increase the feel of professionalism and help the prospects understand it is a business proposal. Also, be sure to never get yourself into a position where you could even be *accused* of false intentions. If you, as a single, are working with a business partner who is married, go out of your way to develop a friendship with the couple together, especially if the excited one of the couple is your opposite gender.

The biggest thing is not to get hung-up on the fact that you're building a business as a single. Be sure and read all of the books that come down through the system, even those dealing with husband-and-wife relationships. This is because you will have people in your organization that will be married, and you'll want to understand and be able to help them. Likewise, if you're married and reading this thinking it doesn't apply to you, you will need to learn to deal with singles that will come into your business. The bottom line is that your business is a people business, not a couples business. Focus on helping others prosper, and you'll do just fine yourself, married or not.

Building out of Town

Building a business at a location many hours from your home is called an "out-of-town" group. Normally, a group is considered out-of-town if it is too far away to drive to and back in a single evening. Subscribers to the LIFE Training Marketing System automatically get unlimited access to a screen share presentation system called "Share Your LIFE," which is designed to allow you to show the business plan to someone at a distance over the Internet. The information in this electronic, online presentation is exactly the same as what you show using the flipchart or sketchpad. This tool makes it easy to determine the interest people at a distance have in order for you to begin businesses out of town. Once they have expressed satisfactory interest, you can then begin to travel there to help them in person. Of course, you can always begin this process by traveling there in person, but the Share Your LIFE tool is available to save you time and money in starting out-of-town organizations.

There are many purposes of building out-of-town groups. First of all, you or someone in your organization may simply know some good people in another town or state. Having a group that is not geographically limited "smoothes out" the effects of localized economic issues. For instance, if the southwest United States has recently been ravaged by hurricanes and the houses in those towns have been blown down, you will suddenly find that rotating the Five-Step Pattern doesn't work so well there. Financially speaking, having a group spread out across the country minimizes the impact of localized calamities on the strength of your business. Next, having groups at a distance will be one of the best ways to learn how to find and develop leaders.

If you can't be there to do all the work yourself, you'll have to learn how to leverage the LIFE Training Marketing System and develop some leaders in that area. This, in turn, will make you better at building your local businesses. Another interesting thing that occurs at a distance is that your credibility is enormous. Prospects think that anybody who would cover a great distance to build a business *must* be committed, and they usually tend to be more receptive to what the out-of-town "expert" has to say. Finally, having groups spread out across the country provides a great opportunity for a little geometric competition. As we like to say, "Competition breeds cooperation." Groups at distances from each other will watch each other and naturally try to be your biggest group. This is healthy and should be fostered, carefully and within reason, of course.

Building distance groups will require a commitment on your part. You are looking primarily for LIFE Members in that location who will do the work when you are not there. If this isn't the case, you haven't found the right people with which to build a distance group. For a distance organization to grow, it will require ongoing feeding. This means that you should travel to see the group regularly. Use the LIFE Leadership events to supplement your actions. In any case, distance groups require a heavy dose of the LIFE Training system. Always arrive with copious quantities of CDs, books, and any other tools they will need to get the business going. The power of the LIFE Training system is perhaps *even more* essential for building distance groups than for local groups: if you don't water the group thoroughly with tools, it will not grow.

You hit home runs not by chance but by preparation.
—Roger Maris

If you want to arrive at your destination, you have to keep the engines running.
—Burke Hedges

Success is largely a matter of holding on after others have let go.
—John L. Mason

You can't have success without discipline.
—Steve Price

If you have a dream and don't follow it, you'll regret it for a long, long time.
—Norm Brodsky

Name: BILLY FAKER
Quote: "I'm doing pretty good. Why
        would I wanna do somethin'
        like this when I'm making
        good money down at the
        toothpick factory?"

CHAPTER 12

CONCLUSION

SEIZE THE DAY

Psychiatrist Alfred Adler said, "The chief danger in life is that you may take too many precautions." Another famous quote says, "To dare not is to risk the most."

Author Alexander Lockhart tells the following story:

> One day, the Apaches [in the time of the Old West] attacked a cavalry unit and captured the army paymaster's safe. They had never seen a safe before, but they knew it held a large amount of gold. But, there was one problem. They had no idea how to open the safe. They pounded on it with stones, whacked at it with their tomahawks, roasted it in a hot fire, soaked it in the river, and even tried blasting it open with gunpowder, but nothing seemed to work.
>
> Finally, the Apache chief had an idea. "Throw it off the cliff," he shouted to his men. This would surely break open the safe when it hit the rocks hundreds of feet below. Much to their disappointment, however, it did not work. All that happened was that one of the wheels broke off the safe.
>
> Totally frustrated, they gave up and left the treasure safe in the ravine. Later, members of the army found the safe, and within a few minutes with the correct combination, opened the safe and found the gold still inside.
>
> Most of us are like that safe. To find the treasures that lie deep inside of you, the right combination must first be found. Once unlocked, you will find the great untapped reserves of potential.

We believe that LIFE Leadership is a lot like the correct combination for that safe. Perhaps you've tried many things in your life to unlock your potential, but try as you may, like the Apaches and that safe of old, you have not been able to unlock your greatness. You have not managed to find the way to take yourself all the way up to your full potential. LIFE Leadership has the ability to unlock all that is in you. But you've got to turn the dial. You've got to use this industry to unlock the safe of golden potential deep inside of you. Remember, LIFE Leadership is not just a plan; it's a *solution*.

A Bike and a Jet

As we come to the end of this book, there is one final analogy we would like to share with you: It is the apt comparison between two modes of travel that we feel goes a long way toward explaining the power of this profession over the lives we were previously living in "corporate America." The comparison is between riding a bicycle and flying a jet.

When we were taught the Industrial-Age mantra "Go to school, get good grades, get a good job with benefits, keep your noses clean, and retire forty-five years later," we were indoctrinated into the world of *bicycle riding*. And we were recruited into this world by a bunch of other bicycle riders. It's not that we weren't making it riding our bikes; we were—kind of. We just had to pedal the bikes we were on day after day, year after year, decade after decade, drafting behind a thousand other bike riders ahead of us in the corporate pyramid.

When we were introduced to the concepts explained in this book, we were brought into a whole new world of speed and maneuverability: flying a jet! But many of our bike-riding associates said, "Look at all those crashed jets! Don't you watch the news? Those things can fall out of the air! And they're expensive! Besides, look at all the progress we're making on these bikes each day. Why, when we catch a downhill now and then, we can hit up to thirty miles an hour! *We're doing pretty well*."

"Yeah," we would answer timidly, "but this is a *really long* bike ride. I mean, forty-five years! We haven't even been alive that long yet! Wouldn't a jet ride be worth it?"

"Aw, I don't know," they'd say. "It takes a long time to learn how to fly a jet. I'm not sure I could find the time to take the lessons."

"But it's a long-term race we're in. So what if we have to invest some time up front. Once we get to travel at five hundred miles an hour, we can quickly make up for lost time!"

"I'll wait and see how you do," they would say.

So we went off to take pilot lessons. Only we didn't have to quit riding our bikes by day. We could continue riding our bikes to pay the short-term expenses of living, but at night, under the cover of "dork-ness," we were practicing to become jet pilots! We don't encourage people to throw down their bikes the minute they hear about this industry and start practicing flying full-time. It's reckless, and it's unnecessary. It's a part-time training system, learned "on the fly," so to speak. (We couldn't help that one.)

Along the way, we saw a few would-be pilots that thought learning to fly was just as easy as learning to ride a bike. Because they had learned to pedal with just a little help from Mom or Dad, they figured they could learn to fly a jet much the same way. "We don't need your training system," they'd say. "We know how transportation works. Have you seen what good bike riders we are? We're just going to apply our expertise from *that*." Or they'd say, "When all my bike-riding friends find out I'm doing this jet flying stuff, they'll flock to the airport to become pilots just because I'm there."

"Okay," we said confusedly. "But we're going to follow this proven LIFE Training system for becoming pilots. We're not so sure we know everything yet, so we're going to listen to those with thousands of successful hours of flying under their belts."

Over time, we never saw any of those "self-taught" pilots flying the friendly skies. That's because learning to ride a bike is relatively easy. Any kid can learn it. But flying a jet must be learned from experts, from people who know how to do it. Flying a jet is not child's play. And bike riders are not capable of teaching anyone how to fly a jet.

"Are you still learning to fly a jet?" our associates would ask from time to time.

"Yep."

"Flown one yourself yet?"

"Not yet. But we're right on schedule."

"Why do you persist?" they would ask.

To which we'd reply, after a pause for effect, "Because no matter how good you get at riding a bike, you'll never *fly* on a bike."

As we began learning to fly a jet, we met others like us who joined us in our journey into the skies. What we discovered is that *inside every person destined to be an entrepreneur is the feeling that they were meant to fly.* Bikes were fine for other people, but they weren't enough for those destined to be pilots.

Once we'd learned to fly a jet, and once we experienced the exhilarating speeds and the fun of soaring upwards in life, we realized that becoming good at riding a bike is much riskier than taking to the air in a jet. That's because if you get good enough at riding a bike, you might grow accustomed to it and begin thinking it's all you were cut out to do. Soaring is for others. You were meant to play it safe on the ground, slow and steady. Besides, it's not *that* bad on the ground, is it?

But once you know you can fly, you'll never be happy riding a bike again.

A Call to Action

We wrote this book not only to teach you how to do something but also to inspire you to do it! Learn to fly! You can do it! Let this book and the information provided within become a call to action in your life. Let it initiate a great season of learning and earning, as well as of living and giving.

Don't blow your shot.

Develop a sense of urgency.

Decide to pursue your destiny.

And never let anybody steal your dream.

Remember this: **Who dares wins**.

If you dare, we'll see you on the victory podium!

We'll see you in the skies!

Conclusion

Never doubt that a small group of thoughtful, committed people can change the world. Indeed, it is the only thing that ever has.
—Margaret Mead

You may have to fight a battle more than once to win it.
—Margaret Thatcher

Obstacles don't have to stop you. If you run into a wall, don't turn around and give up. Figure out how to climb it, go through it, or work around it.
—Michael Jordan

The heights by great men reached and kept / Were not attained by sudden flight, / But they, while their companions slept, / Were toiling upward in the night.
—Henry Wadsworth Longfellow

You look them straight in the eye and say, "Don't tell me it's impossible until after I've already done it."
—Pam Lantos

Name: UNFOCUSED FRANK
Quote: "What?"

While the techniques and approaches suggested have worked for others, no one can guarantee that these techniques and approaches will work for you. We hope, however, that these ideas assist you in developing a strong and profitable business.

LIFE SERIES

Our lives are lived out in the eight categories of Faith, Family, Finances, Fitness, Following, Freedom, Friends, and Fun. The monthly LIFE Series of 4 audios and 1 book is specifically designed to bring you life-transforming information in each of these areas. Whether you are interested in one or two of these, or all eight, you will be delighted with timeless truths and effective strategies for living a life of excellence, brought to you in an entertaining, intelligent, well-informed, and insightful manner. It has been said that it may be your life, but it's not yours to waste. Subscribe to the LIFE Series today and learn how to make yours count!

The LIFE Series – dedicated to helping people grow in each of the 8 F categories: Faith, Family, Finances, Fitness, Following, Freedom, Friends, and Fun.
4 audios and 1 book are shipped each month.
$50.00 plus S&H
Pricing is valid for both USD and CAD.

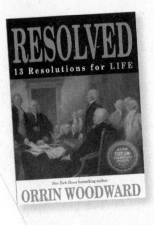

LLR SERIES

Everyone will be called upon to lead at some point in life—and often at many points. The question is whether people will be ready when they are called. The LLR Series is based on the *New York Times* bestseller *Launching a Leadership Revolution*, in which authors Chris Brady and Orrin Woodward teach about leadership in a way that applies to everyone. Whether you are seeking corporate or business advancement, community influence, church impact, or better stewardship and effectiveness in your home, the principles and specifics taught in the LLR Series will equip you with what you need.

Subscribers receive 4 audios and 1 leadership book each month. Topics covered include finances, leadership, public speaking, attitude, goal setting, mentoring, game planning, accountability and progress tracking, levels of motivation, levels of influence, and leaving a personal legacy.

Subscribe to the LLR Series and begin applying these life-transforming truths today!

The LLR (Launching a Leadership Revolution) Series – dedicated to helping people grow in their leadership ability.
4 audios and 1 book are shipped each month.
$50.00 plus S&H
Pricing is valid for both USD and CAD.

Don't Miss Out on the 3 for FREE Program!

When a Customer or Member subscribes to any one or more packages, that person is given the incentive to attract other subscribers as well. Once a subscriber signs up three or more Customers on equivalent or greater dollar value subscriptions, that person will receive his or her next month's subscription FREE!

AGO SERIES

Whether you have walked with Christ your entire life or have just begun the journey, we welcome you to experience the love, joy, understanding, and purpose that only Christ can offer. This series is designed to touch and nourish the hearts of all faith levels. Gain valuable support and guidance from our top speakers and special guests that will help you enhance your understanding of God's plan for your life, marriage, children, and character. Nurture your soul, strengthen your faith, and find answers on the go or quietly at home with the AGO Series.

The AGO (All Grace Outreach) Series – dedicated to helping people grow spiritually. 1 audio and 1 book are shipped each month. $25.00 plus S&H Pricing is valid for both USD and CAD.

EDGE SERIES

Designed especially for those on the younger side of life, this is a hard-core, no-frills approach to learning the things that make for a successful life.

Eliminate the noise around you about who you are and who you should become. Instead, figure it out for yourself in a mighty way with life-changing information from people who would do just about anything to have learned these truths much, much sooner in life. Get access on a monthly basis to wisdom and knowledge that it took them a lifetime to discover!

Edge Series – dedicated to helping young people grow in their leadership ʾbility. ˥udio is shipped each month. 00 plus S&H ˥ is valid for both USD and CAD.

FREEDOM SERIES

Attention all freedom lovers: Gain an even greater understanding of the significance and power of freedom, stay informed about the issues that affect your own freedom, and find out what you can do to reverse any decline and lead the world toward greater liberty with the LIFE Leadership Freedom Series!

Freedom Series – dedicated to helping people understand the meaning and value of freedom. 1 audio is shipped each month. $10.00 plus S&H Pricing is valid for both USD and CAD.

LIFE LIBRARY

The LIFE Library is your round-the-clock resource for LIFE Leadership's latest and greatest leadership content in either video or audio format. And you never have to be quiet in this library!

WATCH, LISTEN, LEARN, AND GROW!

- Audio and video content covering LIFE Leadership's 8 Fs (Faith, Family, Finances, Fitness, Following, Freedom, Friends, and Fun)
- New exclusive content added every month
- Material from industry leaders, including bestselling authors Orrin Woodward, Chris Brady, Tim Marks, and Claude Hamilton
- Option to read reviews and share your own insights
- Ability to create a list of favorites for quick and easy retrieval
- A feature that allows you to search by format, speaker, and/or subject

$40.00 per month
Pricing is valid for both USD and CAD.

RASCAL RADIO

Listen up! You asked for it, and we heard you loud and clear. Now hear this: Rascal Radio is a one-of-a-kind, personal-development Internet radio hot spot. Switch on and tune in to an incredible selection of preset stations for each of LIFE Leadership's 8 Fs that you can customize by choosing a combination of speaker or subject. The life-changing possibilities are endless as you browse through the hundreds of audio recordings available. Select and purchase your favorite talks to gift to family and friends. Listen, learn, and grow through the ease of Rascal Radio.

Subscription includes a 7-Day FREE Trial.
$49.95 per month
Pricing is valid for both USD and CAD.

FREE Rascal Radio Smartphone App Available!

LIFE LIVE

The dynamic, world-class LIFE Live educational events are designed to inform, equip, and train you for success in a powerful way.

Ranging in size from a couple hundred to thousands of participants all across North America, these fun, energy-packed events deliver life-changing information from LIFE Leadership's 8 F categories (Faith, Family, Finances, Fitness, Following, Freedom, Friends, and Fun).

$40.00 per month
Pricing is valid for both USD and CAD.

All Grace Outreach is a 501(c)(3) charitable organization that is committed to providing assistance to those in need. It originally began in 1993 in Maine as "Christian Mission Services." In March of 2007, the organization was transferred to Michigan, and the name was changed to All Grace Outreach. Our main focus is spreading the gospel of Jesus Christ throughout the world and helping abused, abandoned, and distressed children and widows. All contributions are tax deductible.

Mission and Vision: to impact and improve the lives of children both locally and globally and to fund Christian outreach efforts throughout the world.

Here is a partial list of the organizations your donation supports:

Founders Ministries
A New Beginning Pregnancy Center
PLNTD
GAP Ministries
Wisdom for the Heart
Samaritan's Purse
Milwaukee Rescue Mission
Ligonier Ministries
Shepherds Theological Seminary
Zoie Sky Foundation
Catholic Christian Outreach
Italy for Christ

allgraceoutreach.com